George Frideric Handel

Messiah

Leonard Van Camp, editor

Companion Products

65/1001 . . . . Vocal Score	30/1033 . . . . Bassoon
30/1026 . . . . Conductor's Score	30/1034 . . . . . Trumpet I & II and Timpani
30/1027 . . . . Continuo	99/1024 . . . . Compact Disc
30/1028 . . . . Violin I	99/1025 . . . . Performance Cassette
30/1029 . . . . Violin II	*Performance by the Eastman School*
30/1030 . . . . Viola	*of Music Chorale and Philharmonic,*
30/1031 . . . . Cello/Bass	*Donald Neuen, Conductor*
30/1032 . . . . Oboe I & II	30/1004 . . . . A Practical Guide for
	Performing, Teaching and
	Singing *Messiah*

ROGER DEAN PUBLISHING COMPANY

P.O. Box 802 / Dayton, Ohio 45401-0802
A DIVISION OF THE LORENZ CORPORATION

65/1001
ISBN: 0-89328-116-6

Engraved by Gregg Sewell, EditWorks

Roger Dean Publishing Company
Division of The Lorenz Corporation
P. O. Box 802
Dayton, Ohio 45401-0802

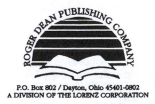

P.O. Box 802 / Dayton, Ohio 45401-0802
A DIVISION OF THE LORENZ CORPORATION

Foreword

This performing edition of *Messiah* is intended to be both scholarly and practical—admittedly a challenge! The autograph score and the conducting score (in facsimile editions) have served as the basis for this edition, and the score by Alfred Mann (Dover Publications) has been very influential as well. I have also studied the Foundling Hospital Parts (a bequest from Handel's Last Will and Testament), the Goldschmidt score (ca. 1749), several early printed editions and scores, and the *Messiah* editions by Clarke (1809), Chrysander (1901), Prout (1902), Spicker (1912), Schering (1939), Coopersmith (1948), Shaw (1959, 1981, 1992), Tobin (1967 and 1972), and Burrows (1987). But the final decisions for what appears here are still based on the two original sources.

The "autograph score" refers to the original manuscript which Handel wrote between August 22nd and September 12th, 1741. The "conducting score" was copied by Handel's amanuensis, John Christopher Smith, and it was used by Handel in his performances in Dublin and London. This is sometimes called the Ousley score or Tenbury score. There are several minor differences in the scores, many of which are noted in this edition. Sometimes the copyist Smith has clarified or corrected Handel's often nearly illegible score in such a way as to supercede it as an authority. But, at other times he makes errors which have crept into many editions which are still in use. Some of Handel's intentions will always remain a mystery.

I have included what some may consider an excessive number of endnotes for a "practical edition." But these are intended to help the conductor who has no access to the original sources and desires to know how editorial decisions were made. There are also many suggestions for dealing with performance details seldom included in choral scores, especially in regard to the length of final notes of phrases. Considerable detailed information and many helpful examples may be found in my companion volume to this edition: *A Practical Guide to Performing, Teaching and Singing Messiah*, also published by Roger Dean. I invite scholars, conductors, and performers alike to study this book for answers to many questions not explained in this edition, or for additional information in regard to details and suggestions mentioned briefly in endnotes included here.

Editorial Practices

There are no **dynamics** in the vocal parts of either the autograph or the conducting score, but there are simply routine *piano* or *forte* indications placed next to the staves for the instruments. To differentiate Handel's markings from editorial ones, *Piano* and *Forte* are spelled out wherever he wrote them. This avoids the use of brackets on every editorial dynamic marking. However, brackets *have* been used if an editorially added term might be confused as being original (the term [*meno f*] for example). Some dynamics have been suggested from other early sources, but those are not noted. The *crescendo* and *decrescendo* marks are all editorial. I have used plus and minus signs (*mf*+ and *f*-) to try to show subtle differences that will clarify choral balance or make thematic ideas clearer for the listener. This kind of dynamic shading has been employed by many conductors, dating, I believe, to Robert Shaw's days of working with Pablo Casals. But it has not, to my knowledge, previously appeared in published editions. To avoid an uncharacteristic extreme, I have used *ff* only twice. The baroque use of "terraced dynamics" is to be kept in mind at all times, but gradations within *forte*, for example, can make a performance more interesting and, hopefully, no less authentic.

The only **marks of articulation** which Handel wrote were vertical dashes, which appear as wedges in this and other editions. These are perhaps more like our current tenuto with a dot (≐) than any other marking we have, although the interpretation of these marks is by no means commonly agreed upon by scholars. Perhaps they also imply more accent than a simple staccato. Any use of the accent mark (>) and the tenuto (−) is purely editorial. I have avoided, for the most part, putting these on strong beats where the current feeling of stress for bar lines or strong secondary accent is already operative in the minds of conductors and singers and therefore needs no additional emphasis. Most suspensions have been marked with the unbracketed sign (< >) as well.

The use of brackets to mark **hemiola passages** will hopefully also be useful. See page 16, for example. In this edition, these appear in many places beyond the usual cadence approaches. Very often Handel's score shows that he was thinking of fewer bar lines than we now use. This is hard to convey in an edition without employing a complicated set of dotted bar lines or some similar device. Several movements have numerous hemiola marks because the music really has less regular accentuation than the "tyranny of the bar line" leads us to expect. In other words—bar lines don't always mean accent, especially in $\frac{3}{4}$ meter, where Handel often interspersed sections of $\frac{3}{2}$, though he indicated no such meter signature change.

For the most part I have avoided suggesting **ritards**, for Handel indicated a ritard by writing the word *adagio*. But there are a few instances where I have suggested that a ritard and *a tempo* take place or that no ritard be taken.

Another unusual marking which appears in this edition for the first time is the "**unaccent**": [‿]. I believe others will adopt this marking too. If properly explained to the performers and carefully observed, it should be most helpful. On page 17, measure 20 of the tenor part, for example, it indicates they should avoid "bumping the end of the phrase" (singing "re—veal—*ED*,") as so often happens. The more customary use of a small *decrescendo* marking for this situation isn't really specific and adequate.

Breath marks (❯) and indications of places not to breathe (＾‿﹍﹍‿＾) have been added to assist in achieving better understanding of the text and more musical phrasing. There are many cases where it is appropriate for the chorus to release a final note a bit early to avoid an unwanted clash of harmony. Such clashes happen because one voice part has a final consonant with pitch (as in G*od*, with it's final "duh" sound) which will clash with another part or the orchestra if held its full value and put in the rest. See, for example, measure 19 of No. 24 on p. 115, or measure 6 of No. 25 on p. 117. These shortened notes can also help the listener hear thematic entrances such as in the "Hallelujah Chorus," measure 69 on page 200. Such final notes have been marked with a numeral and endnoted with the recommended length of note to be substituted.

The few **accidentals** not found in the original sources are bracketed, and some unnecessary ones are omitted.

Trills which appear in the original scores are included and a very few others thought to be appropriate are added in brackets.

Ornamentation has been purposely avoided. **Appogiaturas**, once thought to be appropriate, are not included in this edition since these had been suggested by many editors only because of the erroneous assumption that Handel's operatic practice should be duplicated in oratorio. For a detailed explanation of this whole matter, see Myth Number Seven in *A Practical Guide to Performing, Singing and Teaching Messiah* (pp. 6-7).

The vocal parts have been transferred to the appropriate modern clefs and key signatures modernized. Spelling has at times been modernized as well, and punctuation dealt with in a manner to serve present day performers.

The **keyboard reduction** attempts to supply necessary orchestral lines without becoming too complex. Several passages have been simplified or totally rewritten from the familiar Spicker edition. Long chains of parallel thirds (as in No. 12) and fast figuration in the rage arias (portions of No. 6 and all of No. 40) have especially been avoided. The accompaniment is more idiomatically pianistic, although organists should be able to easily adapt this edition to their instrument. Such keyboard reductions are, of course, a nineteenth-century invention, and are entirely foreign to the original performances, which were always done with orchestra *and* keyboard. Apparently the normal situation was Handel at the harpsichord to play the continuo and an assistant at the organ to double the chorus as needed. In our time, however, when many performances are done with only a keyboardist supplying the accompaniment, such a reduction is essential as well as practical.

A separate **continuo realization** is available for (30/1027) and may be played on the harpsichord (or piano, if none is available) along with the **set of orchestral parts and full score** (30/1026). Or it may be used, where appropriate, to create a kind of **organ and piano duet arrangement** of the orchestral parts. To assist in these situations, a pair of half brackets (⌐ ¬) to show the portions of the score which are *not* doublings of the orchestra have been used. See, for example, page 66, letter A, where the orchestra does not play for three and a half beats. A little imagination and adaptation will be necessary to fit local conditions, but this should be most helpful to many churches and smaller choral societies who cannot secure an orchestra. The addition of a cello (or even bassoon) in such situations will be immensely helpful. Suggestions for the keyboardists appear in the continuo score. And, if a single organist or pianist does accompany a performance, these markings will help to register or voice the accompaniment in an intelligent and informed manner. The left hand part of the Spicker edition is filled with octave doublings that often rumble into the lower register ungracefully, prevent the left hand from assisting with needed harmonic notes, and frequently disguise the outline of Handel's original bass by obscuring octave skips or by moving in the wrong direction. This edition restores the bass line as Handel wrote it, though it may sound a bit thin, since Handel used string basses (which sound an octave lower than written) for much of the work, in addition to cellos. Each keyboardist is free, however, to add octaves or select 16 foot stops where it seems appropriate.

Pianists may wish to "fill out" some of the accompaniment as their experience and fingers dictate, within the bounds of "appropriate baroque practices"—knowing full well that the piano as we know it was not even available in Handel's time.

Modern beaming practices have been adopted for this edition. The commonly accepted slurring of vocal parts has been retained but **keyboard slurs** have been kept to a minimum, and represent, for the most part, Handel's own slurs, which usually indicated string bowings. An exception is "The people that walked in darkness" in which I opted for many additional slurs in a movement where Handel's articulation intentions are especially sketchy. **Keyboard dynamics** follow the plan outlined above—spelled-out markings are Handel's, the others editorial. Markings for **Senza ripieno** and **Con ripieno** which Handel wrote into the conducting score, apparently for one performance in 1749, have not been included in the vocal score. Nor has the presence or absence of the bassoon been indicated. A few suggested **rhythmic alterations** are indicated above the staff, with stems and beams only such as in No. 5. The traditional **rehearsal letters** supplied originally by Ebenezer Prout have been retained, and **measure numbers** have been added.

Each movement has an approximate **timing**, and lists the **scripture** on which the movement is based. A new feature which should be helpful in understanding and conveying the ingenuous way in which Handel set the libretto is the use of **Titles** and **Sub-Titles** e.g. on page 131: [SCENE TWO: THE ABANDONED MESSIAH SUFFERS SCORN]. These are inspired by Jan Peter Larsen's thought-provoking and exhaustive study: "Handel's Messiah", though I remain responsible for their exact wording. In conjunction with this attempt to see Messiah as a series of "scenes", suggestions as to where to pause or not pause between movements have been added. **Metronome markings** are not supplied, because tempo markings (which are more "musical character" indications) are a very personal matter and are dependent on many factors, as pointed out in *A Practical Guide*. Donald Neuen's suggestions for tempi can be found on pp. 203-204 of that book. Conductors and singers are advised to continue to search for the tempo that works for their specific situation, using Neuen's suggestions as a carefully thought out point of departure.

Available Editions of Messiah

In the years since 1948 (when the J. M. Coopersmith edition appeared) it has become possible and, in fact fashionable, to have various versions of some of the movements performed by soloists other than those to which we have become accustomed through the widespread use of the Max Spicker (G. Schirmer) edition of 1912. Handel never did perform this oratorio in exactly the way he originally wrote it in 1741, and he constantly revised and adapted it in the many performances which he produced in his lifetime. The Coopersmith, Shaw, Tobin and Burrows editions offer considerable flexibility for performances, using alternatives provided in an appendix or as second or third versions. This edition, however, follows the lead of Alfred Mann, who, beginning in 1959, gave us what he believes to be "Handel's final or preferred choices for a complete form of the work," based on "the consequences from [Jan Peter] Larsen's findings" (Page viii of the Introduction to his edition, Dover Publications, 1989.)

The movements that appear here are in total agreement with Professor Mann's edition, which also happens to coincide for the most part with the 1912 Spicker edition. The **numbering system for movements** and the **rehearsal letters** used in the Spicker edition (the work of Prout) have been retained in this edition, as they were by Professor Mann. What has not been retained are the many errors which occur in the still widely used Spicker edition. Most of these are pointed out in *A Practical Guide*. This seems necessary because the Spicker edition has acquired the status of "scripture" to generations of singers and conductors who will be quick to point out that any change "isn't the way we've always sung or played it." Thus, chapter and verse have been cited regarding corrections.

We have retained the **pagination** and **layout** of the G. Schirmer vocal score to assist those who wish to convert their choral library to this new edition, but already own a quantity of the Spicker edition. In this way the conductor and singer will still find, for example, that the "Hallelujah Chorus" is on page 193, but they will now also find the correct notes! In the tenor part of measure five, for example, the second note is the F♯ Handel wrote, not the D Spicker printed.

The entire Pastoral Symphony (No. 13) and the complete version of "Why do the nations" (No. 40) have been included so that the page numbering will remain identical to the Spicker edition, though I recommend using the abbreviated version of each. Mann includes only the shortened versions. An "unnumbered page" (181A) has been added to show the way to shorten this latter aria as Handel did on occasion and seemed to prefer. The only deviation from the Spicker edition contents is the substitution of the alto version of No. 36 "Thou art gone up on high" for the bass version, as Professor Mann did.

Acknowledgements

I dare not try to thank all those to whom I am indebted for their help in learning about *Messiah* and preparing this new edition. But I must thank Alfred Mann for his many hours of conversation and follow-up correspondence to answer and then clarify so many questions in regard to both general and specific matters. I hasten to add that he is in no way responsible for any shortcomings this edition may have, nor for the way in which I have added dynamics and editorial markings. And I must acknowledge the very generous help and many insightful comments given me by Donald Neuen of UCLA, who should also not be held responsible for my conclusions.

I also received valuable suggestions and help from Roger Beale and from Jim Walters, without whose encouragement I would never have attempted to re-edit *Messiah*. Larry Pugh, who started the whole project rolling with enthusiasm and my always supportive editor, Scott Foss helped bring this immense undertaking to fruition. My own high school and college teachers, J. Ellis Jackson, Gratia Boyle, Christa Fisher, and Harold Decker taught me to know and love *Messiah*. Some of the others who read the manuscript of my *Practical Guide* and/or made suggestions incorporated into this edition include John Walters, Randall Gill, David Lawrence, David Huff, Ken Jones, Boyd Fees, Patrick Grindol, Jack Overbey, Richard Boyd, Don Shoberg, Conan Castle, David Weck, Andre Thomas, Larry Pounds, Robert L. Brown, Katherine Claudson, Bob Dosien, Richard Reilly, Bob Treat, Jerry Naff, Rod Sturtz, Charles Smith, Jared Faulkner, John Gross, and my ever-patient and understanding wife, Marlene. I thank them all sincerely.

And I especially thank the members of a summer class who studied *Messiah* under me as this edition was in its final stages: Gillian Bertrand, Michael Boschert, James Hannon, Dena Rue, Thomas Schmidt, Jeannine Tiemann, and Raymond Zahra. They made a significant contribution to the quality of the edition and taught me a lot! I welcome suggestions from others who use this edition as well.

Leonard Van Camp

Leonard Van Camp, September, 1993
Southern Illinois University at Edwardsville

Table of Contents

It is requested that all concert notices and
programs acknowledge the use of the
"Van Camp Edition (Roger Dean Publishing Company)."

Messiah
An Oratorio

PART ONE: [THE PROPHECY AND PROMISE OF THE REDEEMING MESSIAH]

No. 1 *Sinfony*
["Overture]

Ca. 3:45

George Frideric Händel (1685-1759)
Begun Saturday, August 22nd, 1741

See pp. 27-28 of *A Practical Guide to Performing, Teaching, and Singing Messiah*, published by Roger Dean, for comments on this movement.

65/1001-3

4

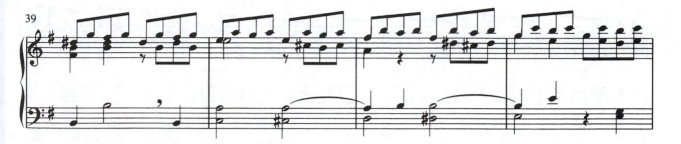

No. 2 *Accompanied Recitative for Tenor [or Soprano]*[1]
"Comfort Ye my people"

Isaiah 40:1-3

Ca. 2:15

saith your God, saith your God.

Speak ye com-fort-a-bly to Je-ru-sa-lem, speak ye

com-fort-a-bly to Je-ru-sa-lem, and cry un-to_ her that her

war-fare, her war-fare is ac-comp-lish'd, that her in-

i - qui-ty is par - don'd, that her in - i - qui-ty is par -

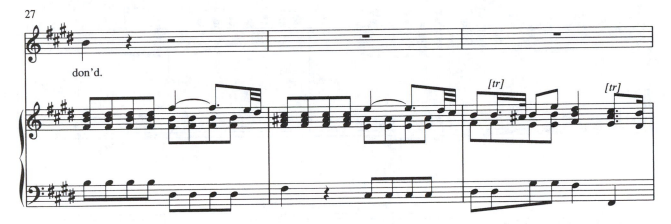

don'd.

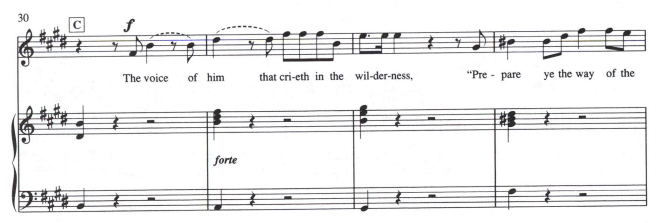

C

The voice of him that cri-eth in the wil-der-ness, "Pre - pare ye the way of the

Lord, make straight in the des-ert a high - way for our God."

[no pause]

No. 3 *Aria for Tenor [or Soprano]*
"Ev'ry valley shall be exalted"

Isaiah 40:4

Ca. 3:15

Piano or Organ

See pp. 31-32 of *A Practical Guide* for comments on this movement.

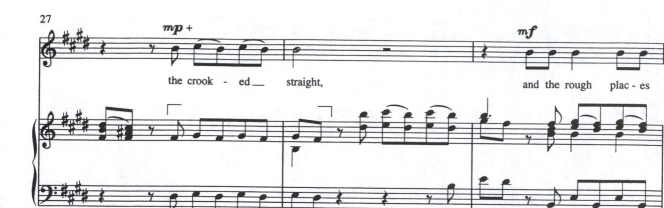

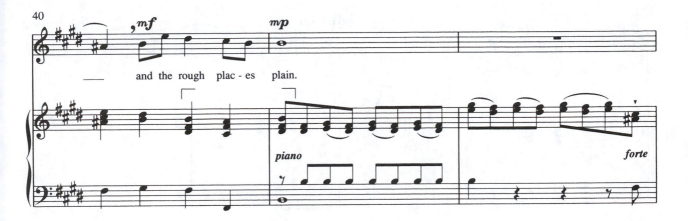

No. 4 *Chorus*
"And the glory of the Lord"

Isaiah 40:5

Ca. 2:30

See pp. 32-36 of *A Practical Guide* for comments on this movement, including suggestions for teaching this chorus and interpretive guidlines.

17
mf
Lord shall be re -
Lord
f
Lord shall be re - veal - ed,
mf
Lord shall be re - veal -
22
f
veal - ed, and the glo - ry, the glo - ry of the
mf
shall be re - veal'd, shall
and the glo - ry, the glo - ry of the Lord
ed, shall be re - veal - ed,
28
A
Lord shall be re - veal'd, and the
be re - veal - ed, and the
shall be re - veal - ed, and the
and the

18

glo - ry, the glo - ry of the Lord shall be re - veal - ed.

glo - ry, the glo - ry of the Lord shall be re - veal - ed.

glo - ry, the glo - ry of the Lord shall be re - veal - ed.

glo - ry, the glo - ry of the Lord shall be re - veal - ed.

And all flesh___ shall

see___ it to - geth - er,

And all flesh___ shall see___ it to - geth - er;

20

22

65/1001-22

[SCENE TWO: THE PURIFYING MESSIAH IS PROPHESIED]

No. 5 *Accompanied Recitative for Bass*
"Thus saith the Lord"

Haggai 2:6, 7; Malachi 3:1

Ca. 1:30

See pp. 36-38 of *A Practical Guide* for comments on this movement.

all na - tions, I'll

shake the heav'ns, the earth, the sea, the

dry land, all na - tions, I'll shake, and the de -

sire

26

No. 6 *Aria for Alto*[1]
"But who may abide the day of His coming?"

Malachi 3:2

Ca. 3:45

See pp. 38-39 of *A Practical Guide* for comments on this movement.

65/1001-27

He ___ ap - pear - eth? But who may __ a - bide, __ but

who may a - bide __ the day of His com - ing? and

who shall stand when He ap - pear - eth?

and who shall stand when __

__ He ap - pear - - - - - -

34

No. 7 *Chorus*
"And He shall purify"

Malachi 3:3

Ca. 2:30

See pp. 39-42 of *A Practical Guide* for comments on this movement.

37

65/1001-37

44

No. 8 *Recitative for Alto*
"Behold, a virgin shall conceive"

Isaiah 7:14; Matt. 1:23   **Mvts. 8 and 9: Ca. 5:30**

No. 9 *Aria for Alto,* and *Chorus*
"O thou that tellest good tidings to Zion"

Isaiah 40:9

See pp. 42-45 of *A Practical Guide* for comments on this movement.

48

up in to the high moun - - - - - tain! get thee up in to the high

moun - - - - - - - - - -

tain!

O

52

53

65/1001-53

54

56

Lord_____ is ris - en up - on thee."

_____ is ris - en up - on thee."

Lord_____ is ris - en up - on thee."

Lord_____ is ris - en up - on thee."

[SCENE FOUR: FROM DARKNESS COMES THE LIGHT OF THE WORLD]

No. 10 *Accompanied Recitative for Bass*
"For behold, darkness shall cover the earth"

Isaiah 60:2, 3

Ca. 1:45

See pp. 46-47 of *A Practical Guide* for comments on this movement.

No. 11 *Aria for Bass*
"The people that walked in darkness"

Isaiah 9:2

Ca. 3:15

See pp. 48-49 of *A Practical Guide* for comments on this movement.

No. 12 *Chorus*
"For unto us a Child is born"

Isaiah 9:6

Ca. 3:15

See pp. 49-53 of *A Practical Guide* for comments on this movement.

68

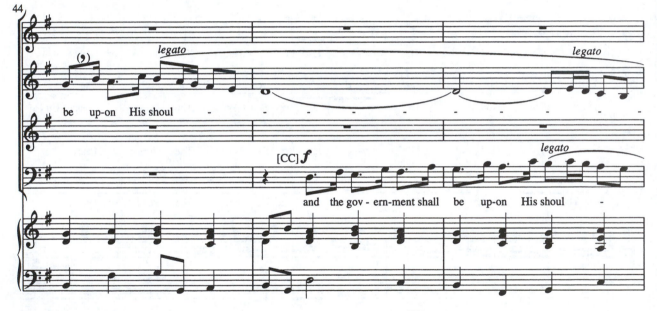

74

81

be up-on His shoul - der, [10] and the gov - ern-ment shall

be up-on His shoul - der, and the gov - ern-ment shall

mf+

mf+ and the gov - ern-ment, the gov - ern-ment shall

and the gov - ern-ment, the gov - ern-ment shall

83

sost.

be up-on His shoul - der; and His Name shall be call - ed

sost.

be up-on His shoul - der; and His Name shall be call - ed

sost.

be up-on His shoul - der; and His Name shall be call - ed

be up-on His shoul - der; and His Name shall be call - ed

85 **G** *f+*

Won - der-ful, Coun - sel - lor,

f+

Won - der-ful, Coun - sel - lor,

f+

Won - der-ful, Coun - sel - lor,

f+

Won - der-ful, Coun - sel - lor,

f+

76

The might-y God, The ev-er-last-ing Fa-ther, The Prince of Peace, The

The might-y God, The ev-er-last-ing Fa-ther, The Prince of Peace, The

The might-y God, The ev-er-last-ing Fa-ther, The Prince of Peace, The

The might-y God, The ev-er-last-ing Fa-ther, The Prince of Peace, The

[poco rit.] *[a tempo]*

ev-er-last-ing Fa-ther, the Prince of Peace.

ev-er-last-ing Fa-ther, the Prince of Peace.

ev-er-last-ing Fa-ther, the Prince of Peace.

ev-er-last-ing Fa-ther, the Prince of Peace.

[tr]

[poco rit.] *[a tempo]*

f

[tr] *[pause]*

S
I
T

No. 13 *Pifa*
["Pastoral Symphony"]

Ca. 1:00 (short version)

Larghetto e mezzo piano

Piano or Organ *mp*

See pp. 53-54 of *A Practical Guide* for comments on this movement.

78

No. 14a *Recitative for Soprano*
"There were shepherds abiding in the field"

Luke 2:8

14-16 Ca. 1:30

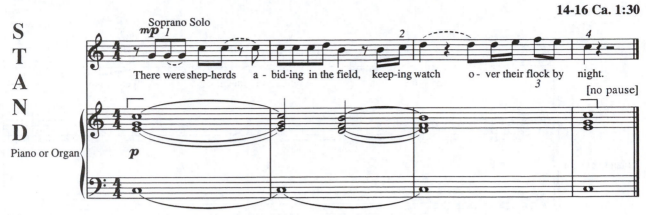

STAND

Piano or Organ

There were shep-herds a-bid-ing in the field, keep-ing watch o-ver their flock by night.

[no pause]

No. 14b *Accompanied Recitative for Soprano*
"And lo, the angel of the Lord came upon them"

Luke 2:9

And lo! the an-gel of the Lord came up-on them, and the glo-ry of the Lord shone round a-bout them, and they were____ sore a-fraid.

[no pause]

See pp. 54-57 of *A Practical Guide* for comments on movements 14-16.

No. 15 *Recitative for Soprano*
"And the angel said unto them"

Luke 2:10, 11

No. 16 *Accompanied Recitative for Soprano*
"And suddenly there was with the angel"

Luke 2:13

No. 17 *Chorus*
"Glory to God"

Luke 2:14

Ca. 2:15

See pp. 57-61 of *A Practical Guide* for comments on this movement.

84

No. 18 *Aria for Soprano [or Tenor]*[1]
"Rejoice greatly, O daughter of Zion"

Zechariah 9:9, 10   Ca. 4:30

See pp. 61-63 of *A Practical Guide* for comments on this movement.

65/1001-87

hold, thy king com-eth un - to thee, be-

hold ___ thy ___ King ___ com-eth un - to ___ thee, com-eth un - to thee;

He is ___ the ___

righ - teous Sav - ior, and he shall speak

90

65/1001-90

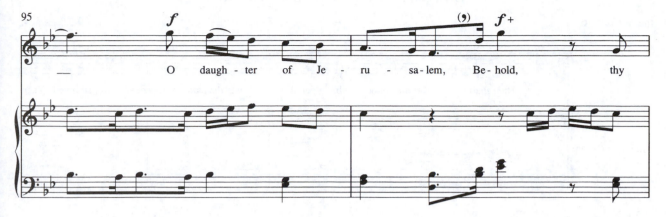

O daugh - ter of Je - ru - sa - lem, Be - hold, thy

king com-eth un - to thee, be - hold, thy king com - eth _ un - to

thee.

No. 19 *Recitative for Alto* [1]
"Then shall the eyes of the blind be open'd"

Isaiah 35:5, 6

19-20 ca 5:45

No. 20 *Aria for Alto and Soprano*
"He shall feed His flock like a shepherd"

Isaiah 40:11; Matthew 11: 28, 29

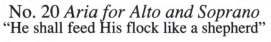

See pp. 63-67 of *A Practical Guide* for comments on this movement.

He __ is __ meek __ and low-ly of heart, __ and ye __ shall find rest, __ and

ye __ shall find rest __ un - to __ your souls.

[non rit.]

Take His yoke up-on you and learn __ of Him, for He __ is __ meek __ and

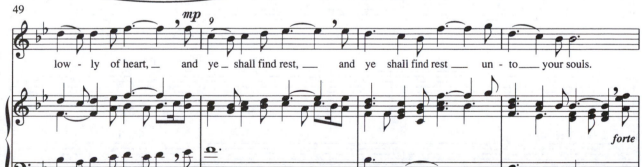

low-ly of heart, __ and ye __ shall find rest, __ and ye shall find rest __ un - to __ your souls.

[no pause]

10 Segue il coro

No. 21 *Chorus*
"His yoke is easy, and His burden is light"

Matthew 11:30

Ca. 2:30

See pp. 64-69 of *A Practical Guide* for comments on this movement.

102

END OF PART ONE

[SCENE ONE : THE SACRIFICIAL LAMB HEALS HIS WAYWARD FLOCK]

No. 22 *Chorus*
"Behold the Lamb of God"

John 1:29

Ca. 2:45

106

No. 23 *Aria for Alto*
"He was despised"

Isaiah 53:3; 50:6

Ca. 9:45 [5:45 with suggested cut]

See pp. 73-75 of *A Practical Guide* for comments on this movement.
*This D.S. is editorial, but is very effective where the full D.C. seems excessively long. A cut may be made from here to bar 36 on the repeat.

a man of sor - - rows and ac - quaint - ed with grief, _____

_____ a man of sor - rows and ac - quaint - ed with grief.

He

was de - spis- ed, re - ject- ed, He was de-

*A cut to this point can be made from bar 11.

No. 24 *Chorus*
"Surely He hath borne our griefs" [1]

Isaiah 53:4, 5

Ca. 2:00

Largo e staccato

Piano or Organ

Sure - ly,   sure - ly   He hath

Sure - ly,   sure - ly   He hath

Sure - ly,   sure - ly   He hath

Sure - ly,   sure - ly   He hath

See pp. 75-78 of *A Practical Guide* for comments on this movement.

114

65/1001-114

No. 25 *Chorus*
"And with His stripes we are healed"

Isaiah 53:5

Ca. 2:00

See pp. 78-81 of *A Practical Guide* for comments on this movement.

120

65/1001-120

No. 26 *Chorus*
"All we, like sheep, have gone astray"

Isaiah 53:6   Ca. 4:15

See pp. 81-84 of *A Practical Guide* for comments on this movement.

65/1001-122

125

65/1001-125

126

127

65/1001-127

65/1001-128

130

No. 27 *Accompanied Recitative for Tenor*
"All they that see Him, laugh Him to scorn"

Psalm 22:7

Ca. 0:30

See p. 85 of *A Practical Guide* for comments on this movement.

No. 28 *Chorus*
"He trusted in God that He would deliver Him"

Psalm 22:8

Ca. 2:30

See pp. 86-88 of *A Practical Guide* for comments on this movement.

134

53
liv - er Him, if He de - light in Him,
sost.
f sost.
in Him, let Him de - liv - er Him, let Him de - liv - er Him, if He de-
f sost.
if He de - light in Him, let Him de - liv - er Him,
sost.
light in Him, let Him de - liv - er Him.
56
f
if He de - light in Him, if He de - light
light
if He de - light in Him, if He de - light
f +
He trust - ed in God that He would de-
59
f + sost.
adagio
[no pause]
in Him, let Him de - liv - er Him, if He de - light in Him.
f +
in Him, let Him de - liv - er Him, if He de - light in Him.
f +
in Him, let Him, let Him de - liv - er Him, if He de - light in Him.
f +
liv - er Him; let Him, let Him de - liv - er Him, if He de - light in Him.
adagio
S
I
T

"Thy Rebuke hath broken His heart"

Psalm 69:20

Largo Tenor (or Soprano) Solo

Ca. 1:30

Piano or Organ

See pp. 88-89 of *A Practical Guide* for comments on this movement.

No. 30 *Arioso for Tenor (or Soprano)*
"Behold, and see if there be any sorrow"

Lamentations 1:12   Largo e piano

Ca. 1:15

See pp. 89-90 of *A Practical Guide* for comments on this movement.

No. 31 *Recitative for Tenor (or Soprano)*
"He was cut off out of the land of the living"

[SCENE THREE: CHRIST'S RESURRECTION AND ASCENSION]

No. 32 *Aria for Tenor (or Soprano)*
"But Thou didst not leave His soul in hell"

See p. 90-92 of *A Practical Guide* for comments on these movements.

No. 33 *Chorus*
"Lift up your heads"

Psalm 24:7-10

Ca. 3:15

STAND

Piano or Organ

Lift up your heads, O ye ___ gates, *and be ye lift up,* ye ev-er-last-ing doors, and the

Lift up your heads, *O ye ___ gates,* and be ye lift up, ye *ev-er-last-ing doors,* and the

Lift up your heads, O ye ___ gates, and be ye lift up, ye ev-er-last-ing doors, *and the*

King of glo-ry shall come in. ___

King ___ of glo-ry shall come in.

King ___ of glo-ry shall come in. ___

Tenor

Who is this King of glo-ry?

Bass

Who is this King of glo-ry?

See pp. 92-96 of *A Practical Guide* for comments on this movement.

146

65/1001-146

148

65/1001-148

REMAIN UP

"Unto which of the angels said He"

Hebrews 1:5

Ca. 0:15

No. 35 *Chorus*
"Let all the angels of God worship Him"

Hebrews 1:6

Ca. 1:30

See pp. 96-98 of *A Practical Guide* for comments on these movements.

154

156

65/1001-156

No. 36 *Aria for Alto*
"Thou art gone up on high" [1]

Psalm 68:18

Ca. 2:45

See pp. 98-99 of *A Practical Guide* for comments on this movement.

gifts ___ for ___ men, yea, e - ven _ for ___ Thine en -

- - - - e-mies, yea, e - ven for _

Thine __ en - e - mies.

that the Lord God might dwell __ a - mong them, that the Lord

160

God might dwell _____

a - mong them, might _____ dwell a - mong them.

Thou art gone up on high, Thou

art gone up on high, Thou hast led cap-tiv - i - ty cap - tive, Thou hast led cap-tiv - i - ty

162

mong_ them, that the Lord_ God _____ might __ dwell _____

a - mong _ them, that the

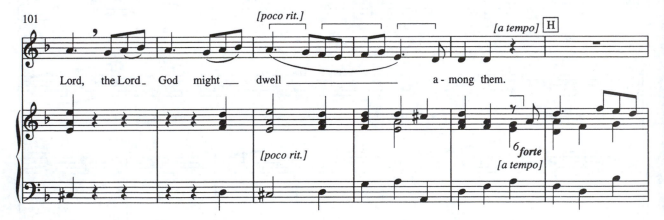

Lord, the Lord_ God might __ dwell _____ a - mong them.

No. 37 *Chorus*
"The Lord gave the word"

Psalm 68:11

Ca. 1:15

See pp. 100-103 of *A Practical Guide* for comments on this movement.

164

*If desired the chorus may remain standing for the following aria to maintain the feeling that all movements of Scene Four comprise an entity.

Romans 10:15

Ca. 1:45

See p. 103 of *A Practical Guide* for comments on this movement.

168

65/1001-168

No. 39 *Chorus*
"Their sound is gone out into all lands"

Romans 10:18

Ca. 1:30

See pp. 104-105 of *A Practical Guide* for comments on this movement.
*The chorus may have remained standing from No. 37.

170

65/1001-170

16
words un - to the ends of the world,
un - to the ends of the world,
mf sost.
and their
18
un - to the ends of the world,
mf sost.
and their
un - to the ends of the world,
words un - to the ends of the world,
20
un - to the ends of the
words un- to the ends of the world, un - to the ends of the
un - to the ends of the world, of the
and their words, and their words un - to the ends of the
tr
3
[tr]

[SCENE FIVE: THE HEATHEN REBEL AGAINST GOD'S GOSPEL]

No. 40 *Aria for Bass*
"Why do the nations so furiously rage together?"

Psalm 2:1, 2

Ca. 1:30 *(short version)*
Ca. 3:15 *(long version)*

See pp. 106-107 of *A Practical Guide* for comments on this movement.

176

34

thing? im - a - - - - -

36

- gine___ a vain thing?

B

forte

39

Why do the na - tions so fu - rious-ly rage___ to -

p

42

geth - er, and why do the

44

peo - ple, and why do the

*Cut to p. 181-A for the preferred alternate short version ending as found in Handel's conducting score.

180

65/1001-180

The kings of the earth rise up and the rul - ers take coun - sel to-geth-er a-gainst the Lord and His an - oint - - - - - ed.

[no pause]

Coro
Let us break
their bonds
asunder

This is the preferred ending of the aria. See *A Practical Guide*
p. 106 for a discussion of this alternate version of the ending,
which Handel may have preferred to the longer version.

Over for Chorus

No. 41 "Let us break their bonds asunder"

No. 41 *Chorus*
"Let us break their bonds asunder"

Psalm 2:3

Ca. 2:00

See pp. 107-109 of *A Practical Guide* for comments on this movement.

184

188

let us break their bonds, and cast a - way, and cast a-

bonds, their bonds a - sun - der, and cast a - way, and cast a-

sun - der, their bonds a - sun - der, and cast a - way, and cast a-

let us break their bonds a - sun - der, and cast a - way, and cast a-

way their yokes from us.

way their yokes from us.

way their yokes ___ from us.

way their yokes from us.

[no pause]

S
I
T

No. 42 *Recitative for Tenor*
"He that dwelleth in heaven"

Psalm 2:4

42-43 ca. 2:15

No. 43 *Aria for Tenor*
"Thou shalt break them"

Psalm 2:9

See pp. 110-112 of *A Practical Guide* for comments on these two movements.

"Hallelujah"

Revelation 19:6; 11:15; 19:16

Ca. 3:15

See pp. 112-120 of *A Practical Guide* for comments on this movement.

194

20
lu - jah, Hal - le - lu - jah, Hal - le - lu - jah, Hal - le - lu - jah,
lu - jah, Hal - le - lu - jah, Hal - le - lu - jah, Hal - le - lu - jah,
lu - jah, Hal - le - lu - jah, Hal - le - lu - jah, Hal - le - lu - jah,
lu - jah, Hal - le - lu - jah, Hal - le - lu - jah, Hal - le - lu - jah,
22
B
for the Lord God Om - ni - po - tent
Hal - le-
Hal - le - lu - jah, Hal - le - lu - jah, Hal - le - lu - jah, Hal - le -
24
reign - eth. Hal - le - lu - jah, Hal - le - lu - jah, Hal - le - lu -
lu - jah, Hal - le - lu - jah, Hal - le - lu - jah,
Hal - le - lu - jah, Hal - le - lu -
- lu - jah, Hal - le - lu jah for the Lord
Hal - le - lu - jah for the Lord

196

197

65/1001-197

198

200

65/1001-200

PART THREE
[THANKSGIVING FOR THE DEFEAT OF DEATH]
[PROLOGUE : THE REDEEMER LIVES]

No. 45 *Aria for Soprano*
"I know that my Redeemer liveth"

Job 19:25, 26; I Corinthians 15:20

Ca. 5:45

See pp. 120-124 of *A Practical Guide* for comments on this movement.

208

know that ___ my Re - deem - er liv - eth.

forte

[tr]

F *f*

For now is Christ ris - en from the dead,

mp

piano

p 4

the first - - - fruits of them that

sleep, _____ of them that sleep, the *mp*

mp

4   G

first - fruits of ___ them that sleep.

p piano

No. 46 *Chorus*
"Since by man came death"

I Corinthians 15:21

Ca. 2:15

See pp. 124-128 of *A Practical Guide* for comments on this movement.

65/1001-210

B Grave

For as in Ad - am all die, for as in Ad - am all die, _____

For as in Ad - am all die, for as in Ad - am all die,

For as in Ad - am all die, for as in Ad - am all die, _____

For as in Ad - am all die, for as in Ad - am all die, _____

For as in Ad - am all die, for as in Ad - am all die,

For rehearsal only

C Allegro

e - ven so in Christ shall all be made a - live, e - ven so in

e - ven so in Christ shall all be made a - live, e - ven so in

e - ven so in Christ shall all be made a - live, e - ven so in

e - ven so in Christ shall all be made a - live, e - ven so in

Christ shall all be made a - live, e - ven so in Christ shall all, _____

Christ shall all be made a - live, e - ven so in Christ shall all, _____

Christ shall all be made a - live, e - ven so in Christ shall all, _____

Christ shall all be made a - live, e - ven so in Christ shall all, _____

No. 47 *Recitative for Bass*
"Behold, I tell you a mystery"

I Corinthians 15:51, 52

47-48 ca. 9:45; 7:30 with cut

No. 48 *Aria for Bass*
"The trumpet shall sound"

I Corinthians 15:52, 53

See pp. 118-121 of *A Practical Guide* for comments on these movements.

*(measure 40) On the Da Capo a cut can be made to measure 108, beat 3, if desired.

65/1001-215

216

trum - pet __ shall __ sound, _____ and __ the __ dead __ shall __ be __
raised, _____ raised in - cor - rup- ti- ble, _____ raised
in - cor - rup- ti- ble, _____ and __ we shall be changed, _____
_____ and __ we shall be changed.

*(measure 108) A cut can be made to this measure from measure 40 on the Da Capo if desired.

and we shall be

changed, we shall be changed,

and we shall be changed, we shall be changed,

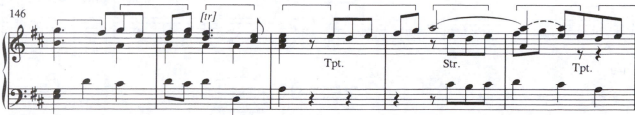

[brief pause
before #44]

220

No. 49 *Recitative for Alto*
"Then shall be brought to pass"

I Corinthians 15:54   Ca. 0:30

No. 50 *Duet for Alto and Tenor*
"O death, where is thy sting?"

I Corinthians 15:55, 56   **50-51 Ca. 3:30**

No. 51 *Chorus*
"But thanks be to God"

I Corinthians 15:57

50-51 ca. 3:30

See pp. 120-124 of *A Practical Guide* for comments on this movement.

226

228

49 (25)

God, who giv-eth _ us the vic - to-ry, the

who giv-eth _ us the vic - to-ry, who giv-eth us the

God, who giv-eth _ us the vic - to-ry, who giv-eth us the

who giv-eth _ us the

52 (28)

vic - to-ry through our Lord Je - sus Christ, but thanks be to God, but thanks,

vic - to-ry through our Lord Je - sus Christ, but thanks, thanks be to God, but

vic - to-ry through our Lord Je - sus Christ, but thanks be to God, but

vic - to-ry through our Lord Je - sus Christ, but thanks be to God, but

55 (31)

but thanks, thanks _____ be to God, to God, who giv-eth _ us the

thanks, but thanks, thanks be to God,

thanks, but thanks, thanks be to God, who

thanks, but thanks, thanks be to God, who

230

65/1001-230

No. 52 *Aria for Soprano*
"If God is for us, who can be against us?"

Romans 8:31, 33, 34

Ca. 4:30

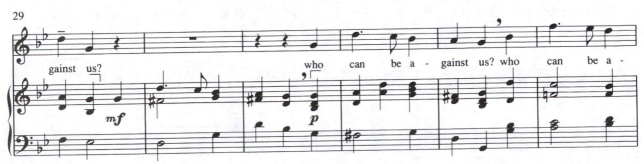

See pp. 137-140 of *A Practical Guide* for comments on this movement.

232

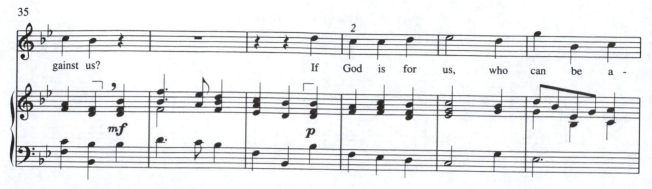

gainst us?   If God is for us, who can be a-

gainst us?

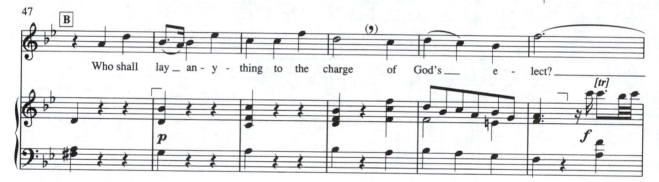

Who shall lay _ an-y-thing to the charge of God's _ e - lect? _____

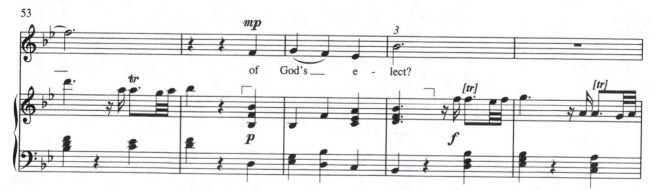

of God's _ e - lect?

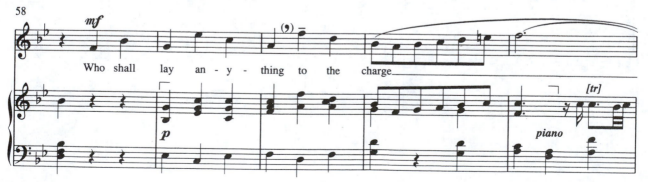

Who shall lay an-y-thing to the charge _____

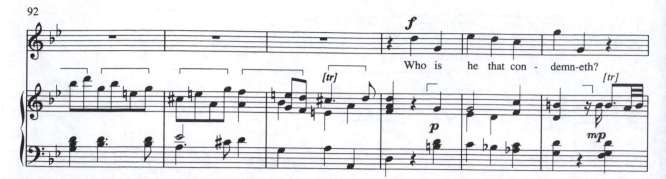

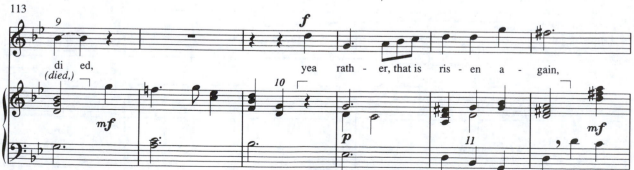

236

146

ces - - - sion__ for us, who is at the

152

right hand of God, who is at the right hand of God, at the right hand of

158

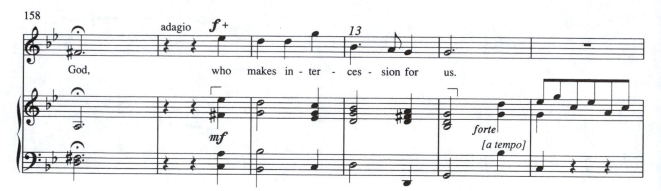

adagio *f* +

13

God, who makes in-ter-ces-sion for us.

mf

forte
[a tempo]

164

[tr]   [tr]   [tr]

169

[tr]   [tr]   [tr]

174

[tr]   [no pause]

No. 53 *Chorus*
"Worthy is the Lamb that was slain"

Revelation 12:9, 13-14   Ca. 6:45

See pp. 140-149 of *A Practical Guide* for comments on this movement.

65/1001-237

239

65/1001-239

41
hon - or, glo - ry and pow'r be un - to Him, glo -
pow'r be un - to Him, glo - ry be un - to Him
Bless - ing and hon - or, glo - ry and pow'r be un - to
Him for ev - er,
43
- ry be un - to Him
that sit - teth up - on the throne,
Him, and un - to the Lamb.
that sit - teth up - on the throne,
45
that sit - teth up - on the throne, that
that
and

*Begin here if cut is taken at meas. 39.

246

[No. 53a "Amen Chorus"]

248

111
H
men, A - men, A
A - men, A - men, A
men, A men, A men, A
men, A - men, A
f
115
men, A
men, A
men, A
men, A
118
men,
[men, A]
6
[men, A] men, A

252

Endnotes to the Vocal Score

PART ONE

Notes for No. 1 *Sinfony (Overture)*

❚ P. 3 ❚

1) All abbreviated dynamics are editorial suggestions. See foreword for details.

2) Measure 12. This repeat is written out merely to match the pagination and layout of the Spicker edition. Handel simply wrote a repeat sign here.

❚ P. 4 ❚

3) Measure 22. Spicker has C♯ here, but the autograph shows C♮. See p. 28 of *A Practical Guide to Performing, Teaching and Singing Messiah* for further information.

Notes for No. 2 *Comfort Ye My People*

❚ P. 7 ❚

1) Title. Handel used a soprano for this recitative and the following aria in a 1743 performance.

2) Measure 1. See note 4 for page 8 regarding keyboard accompaniment.

3) Measure 8. The page of the autograph manuscript on which this measure was written has been lost. The words *ad libitum* are, therefore, found only in Handel's copyist's hand in the conducting score. They probably only mean "take your time," not "freely ornament this."

❚ P. 8 ❚

4) Measure 12. In performances with only organ and continuo (piano or harpsichord) the notes enclosed in brackets are to be played only by the keyboard continuo player (preferably on the harpsichord), not the organist. The organist should, in this case, omit bracketed notes in the right hand part. If no cello, bass or bassoon doubles the lowest notes (basso continuo part) the organist should continue to play these lowest notes as well. In such performances, only the pianist should play these bracketed notes. Local circumstances must, of course, dictate how best to adapt to keyboard(s) this music, which Handel clearly intended be played by an orchestra (supplemented by harpsichord, and perhaps with an organ doubling the chorus).

5) Measure 20. This should be performed as written, without an E♮ added in between. See the foreword regarding reasons for not ornamenting *Messiah*.

❙P. 9❙

6) Measures 24 and 25. No appoggiatura is needed here; the tri-tone interval graphically paints "iniquity." Note that "pardon'd" is only two, not three syllables.

7) Measure 37. The singer should not add an appoggiatura (leaning note) on B here. See *A Practical Guide*, Myth No. 7, pp. 6-7 for a justification of why ornamentation is not used in this edition. Where the note of the singer is not in the chord it is probably best to delay the cadence until he is finished. See *A Practical Guide*, p. 31 for more information on this point.

Notes on No. 3 *Ev'ry valley shall be exalted*

❙P. 10❙

1) Title. Handel used a soprano for this aria and the preceding recitative in 1743.

2) Measure 6. Here, and between measures 7-8 was an extra measure. Each of these has been crossed out in the autograph and pasted over in the conducting score. They were apparently performed in the first performance in Dublin in 1742.

3) Measure 13. The symbol [⌣] is an "unaccent." It means you should "let up" and avoid giving a strong feeling to this final note.

❙P. 12❙

4) Measure 35. Spicker had only "and" here. Handel apparently intended "and the" which can be seen from his use of a beam to connect the first two notes and separate stems for the two eighths on beat two. The conducting score shows three notes beamed and one flagged, but it has been ammended by someone at this point, by adding "& the" as shown here. Further evidence is that every other appearance of these words includes "the." (We have used modern beaming in this edition, of course.)

❙P. 15❙

5) Measure 73. This should not be ornamented. The interval of a tritone itself properly demonstrates "crooked" just as Handel set it. See pp. 6-7 of *A Practical Guide*.

Notes on No. 4 *And the glory of the Lord*

❙P. 16❙

1) Measures 13 and 16. The two syllables "ry of" are to be sung as a single note, as an elision (and as if the language were Italian) but not changed to two eighth notes. The alto dotted half note in measure 14 is best performed as [♩ ♪ ᵧ].

❙P. 17❙

2) Measure 20. This symbol [⌣] is an "unaccent"—meaning the singers should "let up" or "relax" on this final note of the phrase and not give it any stress or prominence.

3) Measures 25 and 28. This [♩.] is best performed as [♩ ♪ ᵧ] to avoid a clash of the sung final consonant on the downbeat against a D♯.

❙P. 18❙

4) Measure 38. This [♩.] is best performed as [♩ ♪ ᵧ] in all voices.

❚ P. 19 ❚

5) Measure 57. This [♩.] is best performed as [♩ ♪ ❳] in all voices.

❚ P. 22 ❚

6) Measure 107. The autograph shows this was Handel's intention, although the copyist did not follow his text underlay, nor have most editors of *Messiah* scores. The dotted slur used here and elsewhere indicates that the singers should not breathe between notes; it may be necessary for them to stagger breathe in order to accomplish this. In that case, singers should breathe in the middle of a syllable, not between words or syllables, so their singing of consonants will not be heard as interrupting sounds to the flow of the remaining singers' voices. The total effect is to be as if no singer has breathed.

7) Measure 110. This [♩.] is best performed as [♩ ♪ ❳] to avoid a clash on the down beat of measure 111 where the sounding of an A on the consonant "duh" sound of the sopranos, would be offensive against the G♯ in the alto. Spicker had a half note and quarter rest here, — an error.

8) Measure 119. The autograph clearly has G♯ for the second note. The copyist made an error in the conducting score here, which Spicker also followed.

❚ P. 23 ❚

9) Measures 124 and 129. The autograph score clearly shows a half note and quarter rest for the bass part in 124 and the tenor, bass and continuo in measure 129. Spicker had them as dotted half notes.

10) Conclusion. This is the place to allow late-comers to be seated.

Notes on No. 5 *Thus saith the Lord*

❚ P. 24 ❚

1) Measure 1. Here Handel's intentions are unclear. It is all but certain that the pickups should be performed as sixteenths in measures 1, 5, 8, 9, 25, and 27 in the keyboard and in measures 7, 8, and 10 of the voice part. These have been changed from Handel's original [❳ ♪] to the now commonly agreed upon [❳· ♪], which he almost certainly intended — a point on which all modern *Messiah* editions seem to agree.

❚ P. 26 ❚

2) Measure 23. Spicker incorrectly printed this G as an F♯.

3) Measure 30. The singer should not add an appoggiatura on A here. When the singer's final note (E) is in the penultimate chord of the final cadence it is possible to play this chord simultaneously with the singer, if desired. See p. 31 of *A Practical Guide* for further comment on this matter.

Notes on No. 6 *But who may abide the day of His coming?*

❚ P. 27 ❚

1) Title. Handel's preference for this aria was for an alto, not a bass. Though the autograph score had a bass clef version, Handel later added this version in alto clef to the conducting

score in his own hand, intending it to be sung by a male alto (*castrato*), Gaetano Guadagni. Thus we have put this vocal part in the treble clef, intending it to be sung by an alto of either sex. See page 38 of *A Practical Guide* for additional discussion of this matter.

▌P. 30 ▌

2) Measure 72. Both notes appear in the conducting score in Handel's own hand, the lower one being slightly larger.

▌P. 31 ▌

3) Measure 93. This editorial fermata is to allow a brief moment to rethink the $\frac{3}{8}$ tempo, and may be ignored.

▌P. 32 ▌

4) Measure 111. Perhaps this fermata should be ignored. See *A Practical Guide*, pp. 38-39 for further comment.

▌P. 34 ▌

5) Measure 135. In Handel's autograph score this occurs at a page break. On the following page it lacks this tie, and Handel repeated the word "He" on this page turn, which most editors have considered to be an error. Spicker's solution—adding a tie and omitting the second "He" seems correct, and has been retained.

Notes for No. 7 *And He shall purify*

▌P. 36 ▌

1) Measure 1. Using a chamber choir [CC] will help to keep the texture from becoming muddy if a large chorus is performing. Handel's choruses were typically 18-24 professional singers, all men and boys, though the female soloists also sang the choruses, as did the male soloists. This editorially suggested "concertato scheme" may be ignored or altered as local conditions and the conductor's preference dictate.

2) Measure 2. All the staccato markings in the accompaniment of this movement are editorial markings which Spicker added, but they are helpful in interpretation, representing as they do the transparent playing of the strings.

▌P. 37 ▌

3) Measure 10. This is the correct rhythm, not [♩. ♪] as is in some editions.

▌P. 39 ▌

4) Measure 21. FC indicates "full choir." This is an editorial suggestion, but one which performance experience solidly validates if local conditions allow for this.

▌P. 40 ▌

5) Measure 27. The autograph has G down to middle C here. Someone corrected this (it makes parallel fifths with the bass) in the conducting score to this now commonly accepted A♭.

Notes on No. 9 *O Thou that tellest good tidings to Zion*

▌P. 49 ▌

1) Measure 29. Both the autograph and the conducting score show even eighth notes here, not a dotted rhythm.

▌P. 51 ▌

2) Measures 64-65. It is possible that Handel intended this series of tied notes to be performed instead as separate dotted quarter notes, viz. ♩. ♩. | ♩. ♩.| ♩. (perhaps even with trills on them). But I have opted for this solution, adopted by most modern editors who assume, as I do, that Handel forgot these ties.

▌P. 53 ▌

3) Measure 103. Spicker had a C here. A is correct according to both the autograph and conducting scores.

4) Measure 106. Handel himself wrote the words "attacca il coro." Literally this Italian phrase means "attach the chorus." Further, he put no double measure here—both clear implications to connect the aria and chorus as a single movement, not make them separate entities.

▌P. 54 ▌

5) Measure 110. Spicker had the wrong text underlay and rhythm here. See example 13 in *A Practical Guide* for verification of this point.

▌P. 55 ▌

6) Measures 115, 116, 119, and 120. Here the [♩ 𝄽] is best performed as [♪ 𝄾 𝄾].

▌P. 57 ▌

7) Measure 129. This [♩ 𝄽] is best performed as [♪𝄾𝄾].

▌P. 58 ▌

8) Measure 132. This [♩. ♪] is best performed as [♩. 𝄾].

9) Measure 133. The [♩.] in soprano, tenor, and bass is best performed as [♩. ♩ 𝄾]. The Alto part [♩. ♩ ♪] is more effective if performed as [♩. 𝄾 ♪].

▌P. 59 ▌

10) Measure 137. Spicker's *allargando* was strictly his own idea.

11) Measure 150. The Spicker edition had two eighth notes here. The fermata in Handel's measure 12, which, on the *da capo* becomes measure 150, is over the top note of two eighths, and a new stem has been drawn so that the first one looks like a quarter. Thus it appears to me that a quarter note was Handel's choice for the final note.

258

Notes on No. 11 *The people that walked in darkness*

❚ P. 62 ❚

1) Measure 2. Only the wedges (vertical dashes) that Handel himself wrote in the autograph appear as wedges in this movement. Many more are implied by the context. The exact interpretation of how to perform these vertical dashes is uncertain. Probably they are close to our modern marking [⸱], indicating some type of staccato separation. But they may also imply some degree of accent. The instrumental slurs are also taken from the autograph, and many have been added beyond those Handel wrote. This solution was reluctantly undertaken despite the general editorial policy of omitting slurs in the keyboard reduction. This was done in an effort to reduce confusion and achieve some kind of uniformity in performances between keyboardist(s), string players and the soloist. Where a staccato dot appears it is an editorial addition that is to be interpreted exactly as a wedge. In this way performers can see what has been editorially added to Handel's very sketchy indications. The slurs in the following measures have been added: 5, 6, 7 (beat three), 9, 12-16, 18-22, 24-26, 28-47, 49-56, 58, and 60--62.

2) Measure 8. The autograph score includes both notes, but the lower ones are larger, probably indicating Handel's preference for them. But if the soloist is more comfortable and effective singing the top notes, he may feel secure in the knowledge that Handel himself wrote them. The bracket below the right hand indicates that in organ and piano (or harpsichord) accompaniment situations the performer playing from the vocal score (which should preferably be the organist) should play only the melody and bass, not the inner voices. This is also true in measures 13-17, and several other places in this movement.

❚ P. 63 ❚

3) Measure 22. Spicker had the slur over the first two notes. Handel wrote it over the E and D sharp, as shown here.

❚ P. 64 ❚

4) Measure 41. This is the way the text is set under the notes in the autograph score and in the conducting score.

❚ P. 65 ❚

5) Measure 56. The autograph score clearly shows Handel wanted the first syllable of "shin-ed" on beat three of this measure. The copyist of the conducting score moved it, however, to the next measure, which is the way it also appeared in the Spicker edition.

Notes on No. 12 *For unto us a Child is born*

❚ P. 66 ❚

1) Measure 7. Since the soloists sang with the chorus in his day, Handel put the word "tutti" here to indicate that all the soprano choristers (perhaps four-six boys?) should sing here, not just a female or boy soprano soloist. But the nature of this music, based as it is on a duet, makes it preferable to have most of the more florid passages of this chorus sung by a chamber choir [CC] rather than by a large chorus. Local conditions and conductors' preference must dictate the best solution, however.

❙ P. 68 ❙

2) Measure 27. The term *legato* used in this movement and elsewhere is always an editorial addition.

❙ P. 69 ❙

3) Measure 33. [FC] = full choir. In the autograph score Handel wrote *Forte* over the sixteenths in the measure before this, which the copyist did not note in the conducting score. Later (1749?) Handel wrote in the conducting score "Con. Rip." (with the full group). But he put this at the beginning of the measure 33. It would appear that an extra group of string players came in only on measure 33, which may serve as a clue to how the accompanist should handle this moment at the keyboard.

4) Measure 37. The wedges appear only in the three upper string parts. See endnote 1 for p. 62 regarding wedges. Whether the conductor may wish for the chorus to observe them as well is a matter of personal preference. The copyist put them in the soprano part in the conducting score, perhaps in error.

❙ P. 71 ❙

5) Measure 51. The autograph has these notes (G, A, G, A) in the second violin, not the continued parallel thirds that Spicker had here.

6) Measure 53. This quarter note is best shortened to an eighth note in all voices.

❙ P. 72 ❙

7) Measure 62-64. Spicker had the wrong text underlay here and wrong rhythms as well.

❙ P. 73 ❙

8) Measure 72. This quarter note is best shortened to an eighth note in all voices.

❙ P. 74 ❙

9) Measure 78. This quarter note is best shortened to an eighth note in all voices.

❙ P. 75 ❙

10) Measure 82. Both the autograph and conducting scores give F♯ (not A as Spicker did) for the altos first note, even though it differs from the second violin note. Such inconsistency is not unusual in Handel's works.

Note for No. 13 *Pifa ("Pastoral Symphony")*

❙ P. 77 ❙

1) Measure 11. Handel seems to have preferred the short version of this *Pifa* after 1743. Measures 12-32 are, in the editor's opinion, best omitted, but are included here for completeness and for consistent pagination of this edition with the Spicker edition. If all 32 measures are, in fact, performed, then this fermata is to be observed only the last time, as a "*fine*" indication.

Notes for No. 14a *There were shepherds abiding in the field*
❙ P. 79 ❙

1) Measure 1. Handel treated *were* as a two syllable word here, as if it were an Italian word: "we-re." Make it like a quarter note. This notation restores Handel's intentions without resorting to Spicker's emendations.

2) Measure 2. The last note of this measure is C, not B as Spicker had.

3) Measure 3. Spicker had the word "flock*s*" in error.

4) Measure 4. The singer should not add an appoggiatura here. Beats 3 and 4 may be omitted with good effect and without doing harm to Handel's dramatic intentions.

Notes for 14b *And lo, the angel of the Lord came upon them*

1) Measure 1. Handel actually wrote "but lo"; the copyist changed it and the conducting score says "and lo."

2) Measure 6. Here is a second instance of "were" set as a two syllable word. Sing it like a quarter. (See endnote 1 in 14a.)

3) Measure 6. The correct notes here are *A* and F, not *G* and F as Spicker had.

Note for No. 15 *And the angel said unto them*
❙ P. 80 ❙

1) Measure 7. Spicker had the wrong rhythm here.

Note for 17 *Glory to God*
❙ P. 82 ❙

1) Measure 1. The autograph score has by the trumpet parts the words: *da lontano e un poco piano*—meaning the trumpets should play from a distance, or literally "off stage". This does not imply that the chorus is also to sing "as from afar" (*mp*) as stated in the Introductory Note of Spicker's edition. See p. 60 of *A Practical Guide* for more on this point.

2) Measure 1. The melody has been indicated through the use of italics in the text, here in the tenor, later in the bass.

Notes for No. 18 *Rejoice greatly, O daughter of Zion*
❙ P. 87 ❙

1) Title. This was the third version of this aria that Handel composed. The autograph has the $\frac{12}{8}$ version. In performances under Handel in 1751 and 1752 a tenor sang this aria.

❙ P. 88 ❙

2) Measure 29. Quarter note is correct, not an eighth note, as Spicker had.

❙ P. 89 ❙

3) Measure 34. Spicker printed a simplified version of these measures. This is the correct notation. In the autograph score, a slur occurs over the fourth beat of measure 35, probably

indicating that "cometh" was to be considered as a single syllable here. Substituting "comes" would be one possible solution.

4) Measure 43. The left hand of beats 3 and 4 are printed as even eighths by Spicker.

5) Measure 44. Handel did not indicate *meno mosso* here as Spicker erroneously printed; the tempo should actually remain the same, though a feeling of "broadening" is to be felt through the singers' manner or delivery in a *sostenuto* fashion.

❙ P. 90 ❙

6) Measure 55. Not dotted eighth and sixteenth as Spicker had.

7) Measure 63. This *adagio* (meaning a ritard, not a new, slower tempo) occurs in the autograph score. Handel then neglected to indicate the obvious "a tempo" or "Tempo I" for the following section. His score is very crowded and messy at this point, but includes "Capo," meaning "back to the beginning," which of course would mean that measure 65 (which equals measure one) and should be at the original *allegro* tempo.

❙ P. 92 ❙

8) Measure 80. Spicker had a B♭ here by mistake.

9) Measure 92. Spicker had beat two as a dotted rhythm. I believe Handel wanted this even, as he wrote in the autograph score.

❙ P. 93 ❙

10) Measure 99. This *adagio* appears only in the autograph, not in the conducting score. Only a slight ritard is recommended here.

11) Measure 101. Handel forgot this natural. See measures 2 and 11 for similar context where he used E♮.

12) Measures 107-108. This probably should be performed as notated here and in measures 8-9 and 43-44 although Handel wrote even eighth notes. The strange situation of this final measure with a bass whole note and a right hand quarter note comes about because the bass line of the conducting score was written out by the copyist (using a whole note) and then Handel personally wrote out the voice and violin parts over it (using a quarter note). Perhaps a slightly sustained quarter note for both hands is the best solution here.

Notes for No. 19 *Then shall the eyes of the blind be open'd*

❙ P. 94 ❙

1) Title. The autograph and conducting scores have this as a soprano recitative and then a soprano aria. This alto recitative and alto-soprano duet version of the aria seems to have been used along with the soprano version from Handel's later years to the present.

2) Measure 4. Perhaps it is best to sing this as a two, not a three syllable word for today's audiences and congregations.

3) Measure 5. The autograph and conducting scores say "a" hart, not "an" hart. Hart is a British term used for a male deer, especially a red deer after its fifth year.

Notes for No. 20 *He shall feed His flock like a shepherd*

1) Measure 5. Do not change this text underlay or that of measure 26 in the way Spicker suggested. This way the singer matches the musical phrasing of the violins. See p. 65 of *A Practical Guide* for further explanation.

2) Measure 9. Here and in measure 15, Handel indicated the text be sung in this manner, not as Spicker had it.

❚ P. 95 ❚

3) Measure 15. See previous note.

4) Measures 21 and 22. This is the way the autograph and conducting score both underlay the text—not the way Spicker showed. The word "those" does not appear in measure 22 of the autograph, but his copyist added it in the conducting score.

❚ P. 96 ❚

5) Measure 25. The right hand harmony on the last chord of this measure is a B♭ chord in some editions. See *A Practical Guide*, p. 64 for a discussion of this matter and the reasons for this choice of an F chord with a seventh. The recommended text underlay here matches the violin part as shown in the conducting score. The soloist should not tie the two F's.

6) Measures 28 and 34. This text underlay appears in the conducting score, perhaps in Charles Jennen's (the librettist's) hand. It avoids a grammatically and syntactically awkward text, and is preferable to Handel's original. In measure 34 the violins, who are doubling the voice at this point have [♩. ♩ ♪]. The soloist, if desired, may also sing that duration and take no breath at this point.

7) Measure 36. In the autograph and conducting scores the voice and violin I (which is merely doubling and has no separate notes) have an even rhythm here, while the violin II has a dotted pattern. A comparison with measures 9 and 15 makes it tempting to dot this, but I have left it as Handel wrote it.

❚ P. 97 ❚

8) Measure 44. Handel wrote "soul*s*" here but "soul" in measure 52. The conducting score has "soul" both places. The scriptures clearly have the plural "souls," which I have retained.

9) Measure 50. Spicker had the wrong text underlay here.

10) Measure 56. Handel wrote these words in a large, bold hand. *Segue* is from *seguire* (to follow) and means here that the following chorus should be started without a break between movements.

Notes for No. 21 *His yoke is easy, and His burden is light*

❚ P. 98 ❚

1) Measure 1. Since the soloists sang with the chorus in Handel's day, he wrote "tutti" here and in measure 5 to indicate that these entrances are for the whole chorus (perhaps 4-6 singers on a part in his day), not just soloists. This chorus is based on a secular Handel duet. To avoid a muddy performance by a very large chorus I have made the editorial suggestion that a chamber choir [CC] sing the more florid portions of this chorus.

2) Measure 3. This was spelled "burthen" in the autograph score, but amended to "burden" in its first two appearances in the conducting score. This seems the best solution for present-day performances, and thus it is changed in every appearance of this word in this chorus.

❚ P. 99 ❚

3) Measure 10. [FC] means "full chorus."

❚ P. 101 ❚

4) Measures 25 and 26. Both the autograph and the conducting score have even sixteenth notes for beat one and beat three of measure 25 and beat one of measure 26. Because of the dotting in the alto in measure 24 and the invariable dotting of this pattern elsewhere in the movement it appears that dotted rhythms were intended here and on beat three of measure 32 as well, where the original sources have even notes instead. Further confirmation that these should be dotted is the fact that these notes are dotted in the corresponding measures of the duet on which this chorus is based. Therefore I have changed them here to dotted rhythms.

❚ P. 102 ❚

5) Measures 31-32. The autograph score has [ ]; the conducting score has the notation given here. Regarding beat 3 of measure 32, see endnote 4 for p. 101.

6) Measures 37-38. This is the way the autograph score and conducting score both show the soprano text, not the way Spicker had it.

❚ P. 103 ❚

7) Measure 43. I believe the text is our best guide to proper dynamics here (as elsewhere) and that a quieter ending makes the point better. Handel wrote no dynamics in any of the chorus parts, and indicated no change in the orchestra parts here, but this *meno forte* has been found to be very effective in performance.

8) Conclusion. It is probably wise to have the orchestra re-tune at this point. A pause is also in order to make it clear that Part One is over if no intermission takes place here.

PART TWO

Notes for No. 22 *Behold the Lamb of God*
❚ P. 104 ❚

1) Measure 1. For a discussion of the "double dotting" that has plagued this chorus over the years see pp. 70-71 of *A Practical Guide*. I believe these rhythms should be performed as written by Handel. In measure three the rhythm on beat one is problematic. When this is later repeated (measure 31) Handel wrote it

264

2) Measure 6. This bass note is a dotted half, not the half note that appears in the Spicker edition. The last note of the tenor is an eighth note, not a sixteenth.

3) Measures 7-8. This is the way the text is set under the soprano notes in the autograph and the conducting scores.

4) Measure 9. Handel and the copyist of the conducting score both wrote singular "sin" as the scriptures also have. Spicker incorrectly printed "sins" in 34 places in this movement.

5) Measures 11-12. It is tempting to have the sopranos sing "be-hold" instead of "of God" on this B♮ and C. However Handel actually wrote "of God." The Goldschmidt score, probably dating from before 1749, has changed this text to "behold."

❘ P. 106 ❘

6) Measure 17. This [♩] is best performed as [♪ 𝄽] in all voices.

7) Measure 18. The soprano rhythm on beat two is definitely even, not dotted, in the autograph score. The copyist made it dotted in the conducting score, an error which Spicker followed in his edition.

8) Measure 19. Not a dotted rhythm as Spicker had.

9) Measure 21. The [♩] is best performed as [♪ 𝄽] in all three voices.

❘ P. 107 ❘

10) Measures 24-25. In the tenor part, beat two of measure 24 and beat two of measure 25, I have restored the even note values of the autograph and conducting scores. In measure 24 the fourth note is not A (as Spicker had) but F♯. I have changed the tenor's rhythm of beat one of measure 25 to a dotted rhythm, which matches the doubling viola part. The alto also has even notes on beat two of measure 25, as in the autograph and conducting score; Spicker had them dotted.

11) Measure 28. I have changed the rhythm here to match the voice part. See *A Practical Guide*, p. 71, for the justification of this change. On beat two, the viola has a dotted rhythm on the same pitches as the tenor part, which has even rhythms.

Notes for No. 23 *He was despised*
❘ P. 108 ❘

1) Measure 2. In the autograph score this is the only trill that appears in this movement. The conducting score doesn't even have this one. The custom of putting a trill on every similar pattern throughout this aria can easily trivialize the otherwise deeply expressive power of this music. See p. 74 of *A Practical Guide*.

2) Measure 8. This editorial D.S. is suggested for situations where a cut in the *da capo* is deemed necessary. One effective solution is to have the soloist begin the last note of measure 8 and sing through measure 11, then cut to measure 36. See *A Practical Guide*, pp. 74-75, for further comment. Another solution to shortening this movement, when it is deemed necessary, is to play the first eight measures and conclude without the soloist singing at all on the *da capo*.

❚ P. 109 ❚

3) Measure 20. The autograph score has A♭ here, which is not only more effective than the A♮ that has crept in over the years, but is, after all, the note that Handel wrote. See *A Practical Guide*, p. 75, for further comment.

❚ P. 111 ❚

4) Measure 49. For comments on the necessity of performing this middle section and a suggested cut during the *da capo* see *A Practical Guide*, p. 74. This fermata, which Spicker failed to include in his edition, is to be ignored the first time, and observed only when the *da capo* is completed.

❚ P. 112 ❚

5) Measure 66. Spicker had even rhythm for beat four. The autograph shows Handel wrote this dotted rhythm, though the copyist mistakenly made it even in the conducting score.

Notes for No. 24 *Surely He hath borne our griefs*

❚ P. 113 ❚

1) Title. The separate movements are not numbered in the autograph or conducting score. It is clear from examining those scores that Handel considered what we now designate as numbers 24, 25, and 26 to be one long chorus, not three separate ones.

2) Measure 1. Handel used the dorian signature of only three flats and then wrote in the D-flat where required. I have reluctantly followed the modern practice of other editors by using four flats and have written in D-naturals as needed instead. The original notation here and wherever this rhythmic figure occurs was [♪ ♫♪. ♪], because the dotted rest had not yet evolved. Scholars seem to agree that it was common baroque practice to perform it as [♪· ♫♪. ♪], and I have so notated it throughout.

❚ P. 114 ❚

3) Measure 7. The superfluous comma that Spicker put in the text has been removed.

4) Measure 8. This quarter note is best performed as an eighth with an eighth rest in all voices.

❚ P. 115 ❚

5) Measure 19. It is better to make this quarter note an eighth note with an eighth rest in all voices.

❚ P. 116 ❚

6) Measures 23 and 24. Spicker mis-read the ties and slurs in the autograph score here. "Was" belongs on beat two. The rhythm in measure 24 is difficult to read, but a careful examination of the autograph shows this dotted rhythm, not two quarter notes, is the proper reading.

Notes for No. 25 *And with His stripes we are healed*

❚ P. 117 ❚

1) Measures 1-6. Editorial suggestion: the words "and with his stripes" should be sung in an accented manner wherever they appear. The words "we are healed" should be sung in a

266

legato manner. If that style is not adopted the breath marks after "stripes" in statements of the subject are best ignored. In measure 4, I have changed the rhythm to an even, not dotted pattern. See p. 79 of *A Practical Guide* for justification.

2) Measure 6. This [o] is best performed as [♩. 𝄾].

❙ P. 118 ❙

3) Measure 13. This [o] is best performed as [♩. 𝄾] to avoid a clash on beat one of measure 14 with the E in the tenor.

4) Measure 14. [♩] is best performed as [♩ 𝄾].

5) Measure 22. [♩] is best performed as [♩ 𝄾].

6) Measure 26. [♩] is best performed as [♩ 𝄾].

❙ P. 119 ❙

7) Measure 32. [♩] is best performed as [♩ 𝄾].

8) Measures 35-47, tenor part. There is no text change for the tenors at this point in either the autograph or the conducting score. Tenors should continue to sing this single word, with staggered breathing, and not make up new text. Handel seems to be indicating the eternal nature of the healing these stripes bring.

9) Measure 40. [♩] is best performed as [♩ 𝄾].

10) Measure 48. [o] in soprano and bass is best performed as [♩. 𝄾].

❙ P. 120 ❙

11) Measure 55. [o] in alto best performed as [♩. 𝄾].

12) Measure 56. [♩] in tenor best performed as [♩ 𝄾].

13) Measure 63. [o] in tenor and bass best performed as [♩. 𝄾].

14) Measure 69. [o] in soprano best performed as [♩. 𝄾].

❙ P. 121 ❙

15) Measure 71. Handel wrote both notes: the upper is better for modern choirs with female altos.

16) Measure 73. This is the correct text, according to Handel's autograph score.

17) Measure 76. Handel wrote only the word "and" here. I believe he intended "are." Thus I believe the text should be "are healed," not "and with His stripes." The text in italics is, therefore, an editorial suggestion I believe fits the character of the music better than that which Smith chose for the conducting score, given in regular print.

18) Measure 80. [o] best performed as [♩. 𝄾] if italicized text is used.

Notes for No. 26 *All we, like sheep, have gone astray*
❙ P. 122 ❙

1) Measure 1. Treat this pattern as shown in measures 1 and 3 each time it occurs. Handel himself wrote the comma between "we" and "like."

2) Measures 4-5. All these purely editorial crescendos and decrescendos are intended to help create the feeling of wandering and restlessness this movement is to portray. Do not make them "Romantic" in nature. Throughout this movement the use of the word "legato" is editorial.

❙ P. 127 ❙

3) Measure 47. These wedges are in the upper string parts, which double the voices here, but are not indicated in the voice parts. They seem to be approximately like today's marking of [⊥] with some implication of an accent as well. The conductor will need to decide whether to observe these in the voice parts as well as in the instrumental lines.

❙ P. 128 ❙

4) Measure 64. Handel wrote both a G and a D for the second eighth note in the instrumental bass. Though the copyist selected D for the conducting score I believe the G was Handel's final choice. The soprano has a dotted rhythm for beat four, though the copyist mis-copied it as even; Spicker also made it even in his edition.

5) Measure 65. Handel wrote both the upper and the lower notes here. In the autograph score the lower ones are larger than the upper ones. Today's female altos should sing the upper notes to keep the imitation intact as was done in the violin I part, which doubles alto at this point.

❙ P. 129 ❙

6) Measure 72. See endnote 3) above, regarding measure 47. The same applies here.

❙ P. 130 ❙

7) Measure 76. This *adagio* is written beneath the continuo part with a lower case "a." It indicates some slowing down . It does not mean "very slow."

8) Measure 85. The only measure lines indicated in the autograph score from this point on are those that are now numbered measures 85, 87, 89, and 90.

9) Measure 91. The autograph score has no text for the sopranos, nor any slurs to guide us. The conducting score has equivocal slurs in the notation, with the word "us" having been put at first on the final quarter note. But then someone apparently moved it to the dotted half, as I have chosen to do. Spicker made a different choice.

10) Measure 92. If an un-cut performance is done and the conductor wishes to divide the work into two, not three parts, this is the best place for the intermission.

Notes for No. 27 *All they that see Him, laugh Him to scorn*
❙ P. 131 ❙

1) Measure 10. Originally written [𝄾 𝄾 ♪♪♩], but properly performed as notated here.

2) Measure 11. It is very effective to omit the final two beats of rest here, using beat two as an upbeat to the next chorus.

Notes for No. 28 *He trusted in God that He would deliver Him*
❙ P. 132 ❙

1) Measure 1. It is curious that Spicker had a "cut time" sign here, when Handel wrote a **C** instead. We have substituted the modern equivalent of $\frac{4}{4}$.

2) Measure 2. Handel wrote "He *might* deliver Him" here and at the tenor entrance. Otherwise he filled in this text only in the bass entrance in measure 58, where he wrote "He *would* deliver Him," which is the form in which it appears in the conducting score, though mostly as an emendation. The use of capital letters for "He" and "Him" is necessary because this Psalm text is used here in what is called "a fuller sense" and refers to Christ.

❙ P. 133 ❙

3) Measure 8. This text, from the conducting score, is consistent with the text underlay in the rest of the movement, though Handel actually wrote "if he delight in Him" in this measure.

❙ P. 136 ❙

4) Measure 37. Spicker had the wrong text here: Handel wrote only the word "let" — a sufficient clue that he wanted the text I have provided.

❙ P. 137 ❙

5) Measure 44. The conducting score has a dotted eighth and sixteenth here, which Spicker followed, but Handel clearly wrote this even rhythm in the autograph.

❙ P. 138 ❙

6) Measure 59. In the autograph Handel's measure for tenors is missing a half a beat, consisting of B♭ and C quarter notes and three eighth notes on F, G, and E♭. This is the copyist's solution in the conducting score.

7) Measure 62. Here Spicker erroneously had the basses sing the cello part octave skip instead of this notation that is clearly shown in both the autograph and the conducting score.

Notes for No. 29 *Thy rebuke hath broken His heart*
❙ P. 139 ❙

1) Measure 7. This trill is not visible in either the autograph facsimile nor the conducting score facsimile from which I prepared this edition. I am grateful to Dr. Alfred Mann for the assurance that it does appear in an 1854 facsimile edition he owns.

2) Measure 10. Handel did not write an appoggiatura here, as appears in some editions.

Note for No. 30 *Behold, and see if there be any sorrow*
❙ P. 140 ❙

1) Measure 2. This appoggiatura appears in the autograph score and should not be ignored. It should receive half the value of the note it precedes and be sung on the beat.

Note for No. 31 *He was cut off out of the land of the living*
I P. 141 I

1) Measure 2. Spicker had an appoggiatura on D here. This is an error due to his thinking the sharp sign was a note.

Note for No. 32 *But Thou didst not leave His soul in hell*
I P. 143 I

1) Measure 31. Spicker erroneously made this a dotted rhythm. The autograph and conducting scores both have even eighth notes.

Notes for No. 33 *Lift up your heads*
I P. 144 I

1) Measure 5. [CC] stands for chamber choir. See p. 92 of *A Practical Guide* for justification for using chamber choir here. The voice part with words in italics should be performed slightly louder than the others to emphasize the melodic ideas in this opening section. For further explanation see pp. 92-94 of *A Practical Guide*.

2) Measure 11. The autograph distinctly shows the text is "this King" five times. The scriptures say "this King." Although the tradition of singing "the King," as suggested by Spicker dates back to the early 1800's, it is clearly incorrect to do so. The bass rhythm on beat two is even in the autograph score, not dotted as Smith copied it in the conducting score and as Spicker showed it in his edition.

I P. 145 I

3) Measures 14-15. I have changed the tenor rhythm on beat two of each of these measures to agree with measures 11, 27, 28, 29 and to match the dotted rhythms of the violin I part which doubles them in these measures. Handel actually wrote even rhythms.

I P. 146 I

4) Measure 19. It is more effective if this is a different group of altos than sing measures 5-18, supplemented by any available first tenors (singing at actual pitch). Measures 18-60 are missing from the conducting score.

I P. 147 I

5) Measure 29. [FC] means the full choir should sing at this point.

I P. 151 I

6) Measure 63. The last note in the alto and tenor parts has been raised one whole step to agree with the strings.

7) Measure 67. It is unclear whether Handel intended the altos to sustain the word "hosts" or sing additional text here. The conducting score indicates to sustain. Most earlier editors favored the sustained text idea, as I do. Some conductors may wish to restore the text: "the Lord of hosts" as several editions suggest.

┃ P. 152 ┃

8) Measure 74. The autograph has F for the alto's last note, not A as the conducting score and the Spicker edition had.

9) Measure 75. Handel does not write *adagio* here. The longer note values are a kind of self-sufficient ritard. The final note is a double whole note and lasts eight beats.

Notes for No. 35 *Let all the angels of God worship Him*

┃ P. 153 ┃

1) Measure 3. Spicker had a G quarter note here. Handel first wrote a G as an eighth note but crossed it out and substituted an E quarter note. This is also the note for the doubling viola. The conducting score also has an E here.

┃ P. 154 ┃

2) Measure 10. Handel wrote both a high and a low D here, probably because the male altos who made up his performance choirs might not be able to sing the high note, but the female soloist could. He made a point of indicating that the violin II should play the upper note—showing it to be his preference. All female altos of today who can should sing the higher note.

┃ P. 155 ┃

3) Measure 15. Handel wrote both a high and a low A here. That the upper one is his preference can be shown by the fact that he made a point of having the doubling violas play the higher note. But second tenors may sing the lower notes with his blessing. (Some altos could help out on the high A here, too.)

┃ P. 156 ┃

4) Measure 27. Handel wrote not only the low A, which Spicker printed, but also a high A, which most early editors failed to notice because the stem looks like a part of the word "him" in the alto.

Notes for No. 36 *Thou art gone up on high*

┃ P. 158 ┃

1) Title. This is the one departure from the Spicker edition's contents. He selected the bass version of this aria from the autograph score—a version which Handel probably never performed. This alto version included here is similar to the bass version but is 28 measures shorter. It was written for Gaetano Guadagni, probably in 1750, and later bound into the conducting score, where it can be found today. The feeling of $\frac{3}{2}$, not $\frac{3}{4}$ permeates the opening measures — as if the measure lines for measures 2, 4, 6, 8, and 10 were not present. This same feeling (hemiola) exists in much of this movement. Only a few such places have been indicated.

2) Measure 15. Dynamic taken from the corresponding measure in the bass version.

┃ P. 159 ┃

3) Measure 37. Dynamic taken from the corresponding measure (33) of the bass version.

❚ P. 160 ❚

4) Measure 52. Handel wrote a flat in front of the B here. It is possible he meant a natural instead since he also wrote a flat in front of the B that begins the next measure; both accidentals would actually be unnecessary had he not wanted a B♮ in measure 52. I have left it as he wrote it—B♭.

5) Measure 56. Dynamic taken from the corresponding measure (51) of the bass version.

❚ P. 162 ❚

6) Measure 105. Dynamic from corresponding measure (112) of bass version.

Notes for No. 37 *The Lord gave the word*

❚ P. 164 ❚

1) Measure 9. This fermata is editorial, but has proven effective in performance.

2) Measure 10. This [♩] is best performed as [♩. 𝄾].

Notes for No. 38 *How beautiful are the feet*

❚ P. 167 ❚

1) When the accompaniment is done as an organ and piano duet, the organist should play only the violin's melodic line (top notes), and the lowest note of the left hand part (which duplicates the cello and bass part) through measure 4. The pianist (or perhaps it is a harpsichordist) will be playing the continuo part (available separately) and will fill in the harmonies shown there. Similarly, in measures 7-10, it will be better to play only the lowest sounding notes of the left hand (cello, that is) and to omit all but the melodic line (highest note) of the right hand part. Measures 13 (and pickup) to 19 (beat 3), should be similarly treated, as should 21 (and pickup) to the end. That leaves two places where the organist should play only the left hand (cello) notes: measure 11 (and pickup) to beat three of measure 12, and measure 19, beat four, through all but the last two notes of the final measure.

Notes for No. 39 *Their sound is gone out into all lands*

❚ P. 170 ❚

1) Measure 10. Both the autograph and conducting score have a G here. But this A♭ agrees with the oboe II and violin II parts which are doubling the altos.

2) Measure 11. Spicker had the wrong bass rhythm here, copying the vocal rhythm, whereas Handel wrote this bass part for the instruments.

❚ P. 171 ❚

3) Measure 22. Spicker incorrectly had a dotted rhythm here.

❚ P. 172 ❚

4) Measure 29. The autograph score has this text. The copyist changed it to "and their words." I believe Handel's choice was correct, based on the musical context, since the soprano and alto are moving together and the tenor and bass are relatively static, thus suggesting the repeated, not the new words for tenors.

272

❙P. 173❙

5) Measure 37. Spicker had the vocal, rather than these correct instrumental rhythms here.

Notes for No. 40 *Why do the nations so furiously rage together?*

❙P. 174❙

1) Measure 1. The keyboard reduction has been considerably revised from the Spicker version in an attempt to make it playable by more keyboardists.

❙P. 175❙

2) Measure 19. Handel's autograph score is blurred here. He may have intended a B, but almost all sources have assumed A to be correct.

❙P. 181❙

3) Measure 83. This is the way Handel seemed to want this word divided. He actually spelled it "counsels" here and in measure 82 as well, and the copyist did so every time in the conducting score. Scripture clearly says "counsel." The word refers to meeting "in counsel," that is to say, meeting in a conference together to plot, scheme or conspire. He used the same plural form of the word in the short recitative version which is on the next page.

Notes for No. 41 *Let us break their bonds asunder*

❙P. 183❙

1) Measure 8. Spicker mistakenly had the basses sing the same text as the upper voices here. This text underlay follows the autograph and the conducting score.

2) Measure 16. Handel did not tie this pattern in the violin parts as he did in the voices. The written out continuo part (in alto clef) does have ties in measures 11-14, however. Where ties are omitted, the repeated note can help to keep the singers from rushing and also contribute to the rhythmic vitality of this movement.

❙P. 184❙

3) Measures 20-21. Handel forgot to put a sharp in front of the F's in these measures in the string parts.

❙P. 185❙

4) Measure 32. Handel may have intended a G in the tenor, not a quarter rest here. I am following the conducting score in using the rest.

Notes for No. 43 *Thou shalt break them*

❙P. 189❙

1) Measure 1. Spicker included dozens of wedge-shaped "staccato marks" which neither Handel nor his copyist indicated. These have been removed. Instead, only those indicated by Handel in the autograph score as vertical dashes appear here as wedges, and those I have editorially supplied (some of which agree with Spicker) appear as the more modern dots. The notes with dots should be performed as though they are wedges, if the performers agree with my editorial judgement, or otherwise should be omitted. See pp. 111-112 of *A Practical Guide* for more information on this point.

When this movement is done without orchestra, in an organ and piano (or harpsichord) duet version of the accompaniment, the organist should play the top notes of the right hand and the two eighth notes that are usually shown in the left hand on the and of three and the down beat of the next measure, since this represents the unison violins. The organist may also play the left hand chords, or at least the lowest sounding pitch, which represents the cello and bass part. A bracket appearing below the right hand part (as in measures 8-10) or above the bass clef (as in measures 22-23) indicates that the other keyboardist, playing from the continuo part (available separately), will cover the harmonies at that point, and the organist should concentrate on the dramatic violin and cello/bass parts only.

❙P. 190❙

2) Measure 26. Here, for 7½ beats, the left hand part alone represents what Handel actually wrote for strings. The right hand part represents a continuo realization, and can perhaps be omitted when only one keyboardist is accompanying the soloist.

3) Measure 32. Here Smith, the copyist of the conducting score, put a wedge (vertical dash) over the last note of the measure, and the first notes of the next, which has a slur as well; an obvious inconsistency. I have omitted both dashes.

❙P. 191❙

4) Measure 38. Spicker and some other editors have taken this measure from the conducting score, not the autograph. Their editions have different (higher) notes here. This is the correct reading. See p. 112 of *A Practical Guide* for details regarding this measure.

5) Measures 44-48. From the last note in measure 44 through measure 48 the left hand part represents the string parts Handel wrote. The right hand part may be eliminated when only one keyboardist is playing.

❙P. 192❙

6) Measure 63. Spicker had [♩ ♫] here in error. Both the autograph and conducting score show this rhythm instead.

7) Measure 74. This is measure 10 in the *da capo* which Handel indicated at this point in the autograph. The fermatas included there are only to make clear where to stop at the end and have therefore not been included here, in either measure 10 or measure 74.

Notes for No. 44 *Hallelujah Chorus*
❙P. 193❙

1) Measure 4. Handel uses a musical motive ("so-la-so") in this chorus more than 50 times. The voice part given this motive has its text set in italics throughout this movement as a reminder to emphasize it slightly. See *A Practical Guide*, pp. 114-115, for further discussion on this.

When this movement is done without orchestra in an organ and piano (or harpsichord) duet version of the accompaniment, the organist should play only the stems-up notes of the right hand. The organist may also play the left hand chords, or at least the lowest sounding pitch, which represents the cello and bass part. A bracket appearing below the right hand part (as in measures 4-6) indicates that the other keyboardist, playing from the continuo part (available separately) will cover the harmonies at that point.

2) Measure 5. Both the autograph and the conducting score have F♯, not D, for the tenors' second note.

❙ P. 195 ❙

3) Measures 23 and 24. Here and in several other places, Handel indicates only a single note for two syllables of text. This notation is a result of Handel's familiarity with Italian rather than English since he wrote his operas in Italian. Do not attempt to sing two sixteenth notes, but elide the two syllables to fit together in the space of one note.

4) Measure 25. This is not an elision. Two separate notes must be sung with separate syllables of text.

❙ P. 196 ❙

5) Measure 26. The tie is in the autograph and conducting score. Spicker mis-read Handel's intentions here. Also see note 3 regarding measure 23.

6) Measures 30-31. See note 3 regarding measure 23.

❙ P. 197 ❙

7) Measure 32. See note 3 regarding measure 23.

8) Measure 33. Neither the autograph nor conducting score suggests that the tempo should slow down here nor that the voices should sing piano, as has been done traditionally without any apparent authority.

9) Measure 38. Handel first wrote a G here, then crossed it out and wrote D. He put G instead in the tenor, apparently to avoid parallel fifths with the soprano. It should be clearly heard as if it were a note in the altos statement of the theme, as the sopranos had it in measure 34 and as the violins and trumpets have simultaneously with this alto statement. The sopranos complete the statement in measures 40 and 41. See example 69, p. 116 in *A Practical Guide*.

10) Measure 41. The [♩] in soprano, alto, and tenor is best performed as [♩. 𝄾]. In the bass part [♩. ♪] is best performed as [♩ 𝄾 ♪].

❙ P. 198 ❙

11) Measure 43. Handel wrote a trill over this bass note—the only such choral trill in the work. I believe it is best ignored, although I have had choruses execute it. If this trill is performed, then other statements of this theme probably need a trill as well.

12) Measure 46. Handel wrote only the lower note for his male altos, for whom the upper D was very high. But in measure 79 he wrote both the upper and lower D. The upper note gives the theme its proper outline, as it is performed by the violin II and viola here. Someone—it could have been Handel—pencilled in a note-head but no stem here in the conducting score.

❚ P. 199 Score ❚

13) Measure 51. [♩] in soprano is best performed as [♩𝄽].

14) Measure 57. Sopranos cut-off on 1, but altos hold until beat three.

❚ P. 200 ❚

15) Measure 60. Soprano [♩] best performed as [𝄽].

16) Measure 63. Soprano [♩] best performed as [♩𝄽].

17) Measure 66. Soprano [♩.] best performed as [♩𝄾].

18) Measure 69. Soprano, alto, and tenor [♩] best performed as [♩. 𝄾]. The bass [♩.] is best done as [♩𝄾].

❚ P. 201 Score ❚

19) Measure 76. I think Handel may have intended this text to be "And he shall reign," but this traditionally hallowed reading has been preserved here. See p. 118 of *A Practical Guide*.

❚ P. 202 Score ❚

20) Measure 79. Handel wrote both notes; the upper is preferred, to properly state the theme. The next note is A in both the autograph and the conducting score; nearly every editor has assumed, as I do, that Handel meant F♯, to match the theme, and to avoid an open fifth.

21) Measure 81. The last sixteenth note of beat three is D, not E as Spicker had. It is effective to drop the dynamics back to *mf* here in order to then build to a fuller ending.

22) Measure 94. Perhaps the orchestra will need to re-tune at this point.

PART THREE

Notes for No. 45 *I know that my Redeemer liveth*
❚ P. 205 ❚

1) Measure 44, and measures 57-59. This is Handel's text underlay in the autograph score. See comments in *A Practical Guide to Performing, Teaching and Singing Messiah*, pp. 122-23, for further comment on the whole matter of text underlay in this movement.

❚ P. 206 ❚

2) Measures 64-66. Spicker had wrong rhythms in each of these measures. The autograph and conducting score both show the notation printed here to be correct.

❚ P. 207 ❚

3) Measure 84. This initial note is an eighth in the autograph and in the conducting score and not a sixteenth as Spicker printed.

❚ P. 208 ❚

4) Measures 125-128 and 135-136. This is the way Handel set this text in the autograph. See p. 123 of *A Practical Guide*.

I P. 209 I

5) Measures 150-153. This is the way Handel set this text in the autograph. The proper placement of the word "that" is unclear; I believe this to be the best solution, but would accept it being sung on the final eighth instead. The final note was a dotted half, not a half as printed by Spicker.

Notes for No. 46 *Since by man came death*

I P. 210 I

1) Measure 1. The pitch should be given softly but clearly by only the continuo keyboardist. No cello or bass should play, and the orchestra should not play the chord, unless there is no keyboardist.

I P. 212 I

2) Measure 17. Spicker had a quarter note value here; Handel wrote a half note, as did the copyist of the conducting score. Only one keyboardist should give this pitch, as outlined in the previous endnote.

I P. 213 I

3) Measure 29. The additional text which the Spicker edition added here, though dating back to at least the early 19th century, is definitely not authentic. This is how Handel wanted the basses to sing this "resurrection" passage. See comments and musical example 77 on p. 127 of *A Practical Guide*.

Notes for No. 47 *Behold, I tell you mystery*

I P. 214 I

1) Measure 5. Handel spelled the word "chang'd," perhaps to show it was not a two syllable word: "chang-ed." I have adopted the modern spelling here and in the following aria as well.

2) Measure 7. Spicker had an eighth rest here.

3) Measure 8. See p. 129 of *A Practical Guide*, example 79, for a way to handle this transition.

Notes for No. 48 *The trumpet shall sound*

1) Measures 1-3. Some scholars and performers believe the rhythmic pattern [♩ 𝄽 ♫. ♪] or [♩. ♫♪] should be played [♩ 𝄽. ♫. ♪] here and similarly in measures 31-33, 47-49, 85-89, and 141-143.

I P. 215 I

2) Measures 17-20. Some scholars and performers believe these measures should be played [♩. ♫. ♫. ♪].

3) Measure 31. Spicker had a dotted half note here in error.

4) Measure 34. Handel spelled it "rais'd" throughout.

5) Measure 38. See *A Practical Guide*, p. 131, for a discussion of the problem of this textual underlay. Also see note 7, below.

▮P. 216▮

6) Measure 48. Spicker had an eighth rest here by mistake.

7) Measures 51-56 (which uses different pitches), and 91-96. Handel wrote:

8) Measure 58. Spicker had an A here; this is clearly an error, though one of long-standing.

▮P. 217▮

9) Measures 91-96. See end note 7, above.

▮P. 218▮

10) Measure 118. Spicker omitted the word "and" here.

▮P. 219▮

11) Measures 138-139 and measure 156. Ignore the fermata and *adagio* instruction the first time, if the middle section and *da capo* are to be done. In measure 156, ignore the fermata the first time.

▮P. 220▮

12) Measures 182-194. This entire section for the soloist feels as if it is actually in $\frac{3}{2}$, with every other bar line being "removed."

▮P. 221▮

13) Measure 186. The slurs on this page are merely editorial suggestions.

14) Measure 211. Spicker failed to print *adagio* here.

Note for No. 49 *Then shall be brought to pass*

▮P. 222▮

1) Measure 5. This is best done as a "simultaneous" cadence, and not delayed until the singer as finished.

Notes for No. 50 *O death, where is thy sting?*

1) Measure 5. Handel rarely wrote in the conducting score. But he wrote these three notes and indicated (by pasting over) that a cut was to be made to measure 23, which has now become measure 6 in almost all editions, including Spicker's.

▮P. 223▮

2) Measure 12. Here Handel wrote [♩. ♪ 𝄾 ♩ ♩]. His copyist changed it to read as shown here, which almost all editors have accepted through the years.

▮P. 224▮

3) Measure 16. Spicker had B♭ as the second note here. Handel and his copyist both had an A♭. The harmonic context makes it all but certain A♮ was the intended note.

4) Measure 24. Handel put no double bar lines here. He thought of the duet and chorus as a single movement, as is shown by his words "segue chorus." Therefore, there should be no hesitation before beginning the chorus.

Notes for No. 51 *But thanks be to God*

❙ P. 225 ❙

1) Measure 1. The extra set of measure numbers used here will assist performers if other editions or orchestral parts are used.

❙ P. 226 ❙

2) Measure 31. The alto text underlay here is uncertain. I believe this to be the best solution.

3) Measure 38. This is the way the autograph score has the text underlayed.

❙ P. 228 ❙

4) Measure 49. The [𝅗𝅥] is best performed as [𝅘𝅥. 𝄿 in the soprano and tenor.

5) Measure 52. Handel's spelling, "thro'," has been modernized throughout.

❙ P. 229 ❙

6) Measure 58. Spicker had a B♭ here. D is the correct note, as shown by the autograph and the conducting score.

7) Measure 61. The autograph has a C here, corrected by the copyist in the conducting score to agree with violin I.

Notes for No. 52 *If God is for us, who can be against us?*

❙ P. 231 ❙

1) Measure 25. This is the way Handel wrote this, with the exception that I have used "is" rather than "be," as Handel did in measure 38. Someone also changed the conducting score to "is" in both places. However, I have retained his rhythmic setting to match the melody introduced in measures 1-3. See *A Practical Guide*, pp. 138-139, for further discussion. Spicker and most others take the reading as revised in the conducting score.

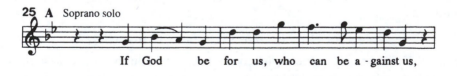

❙ P. 232 ❙

2) Measure 38. Handel wrote "If God *is* for us" (italics mine) and used this notation. Spicker and others revised it.

3) Measure 56. Not a half note and quarter rest, as Spicker had.

❙ P. 233 ❙

4) Measure 69. This is correctly a rest, not a C minor first inversion triad, as Spicker had.

5) Measure 73. Both the autograph and conducting score have a half note for the violins and a quarter note for the basso continuo.

6) Measure 89. This is from the autograph. The copyist incorrectly put the rhythm [♪. ♫♪♪♪], as did Spicker.

❙ P. 234 ❙

7) Measures 101 and 103. The Spicker edition incorrectly had even rhythms in both of these measures. Both the autograph and conducting scores clearly show the rhythms shown here.

8) Measure 107. Handel wrote a half note and quarter rest, not a dotted half as Spicker had.

9) Measures 113-115. The autograph and conducting scores both show two quarters and the word "died," written without a hyphen. Handel probably thought of it as pronounced by Italian rules: "di-ed." In modern performances it is preferable to sing it as a half note and a single syllable. The left hand rhythm in measure 113 is incorrect in the Spicker [♩ ♩].

10) Measure 115. The correct note in both the autograph and conducting score is G, not the B♭ that Spicker had.

11) Measure 117. Spicker had a C for the 2nd bass note. B♭ is the note Handel wrote and Smith copied into the conducting score.

❙ P. 235 ❙

12) Measure 123. Handel wrote a half note and a quarter rest, which the copyist, Smith, made a dotted half in the conducting score. Spicker had adopted Smith's solution—but I have restored Handel's choice.

❙ P. 236 ❙

13) Measures 161-162. Handel wrote the notes that appear here. Spicker made this measure "harmonize" but gave the wrong notes. Though Handel wrote a dotted half for the final notes, it may be advisable in some situations to shorten the last note to a half note and add a quarter rest so the final consonant is heard before the instrumental *ritornello* is played. Spicker actually printed this measure that way. The clash of the soloist's G with the A in the continuo part is not an error, but an example of the "Corelli clash", as happens again in measure 177.

Notes for No. 53 *Worthy is the Lamb that was slain*
❙ P. 237 ❙

1) Measure 1. Here the melody is split between the tenor and alto. Compare with soprano at letter A.

❙ P. 239 ❙

2) Measure 24. An elision, not two separate sixteenth notes, is required here and in all similar measures. See endnote 3 for p. 195.

▮ P. 241 ▮

3) Measure 39. Donald Burrows says Handel made this cut for the 1743 performance. It appears as a revision in the autograph score. See *A Practical Guide*, pp. 145-146 for comments.

▮ P. 245 ▮

4) Measure 60. Spicker had the wrong note here (an F♯).

5) Measure 62. Spicker had "for" in the alto, tenor, and bass here. The autograph and the conducting score both show "and."

Notes on No. 53a *Amen Chorus*
▮ P. 247 ▮

1) Measures.78-80. These wedges appear as vertical dashes in the autograph score, here and in other measures. (See endnote 1 for p. 62 regarding wedges.) The copyist of the conducting score added a few wedges, which I have not included. The addition of text to these measures as was done in the Spicker edition is absolutely incorrect. See example 93, p. 150 of *A Practical Guide* for proof of this fact.

2) Measure 80. Neither the autograph score nor the conducting score indicate that Handel wanted text added here. But the comparison with measures 75 (bass), 85 (alto), 105 (bass), and 112 (bass) seem to indicate that this was an oversight.

▮ P. 248 ▮

3) Measure 103. Here Handel put wedges over all three notes, not just the first two as he had done in measures 88 and 89.

4) Measure 106. [♩] best performed as [♩.𝄾] in all voices.

5) Measure 109. This text underlay for alto is clearly shown in the autograph score, though the copyist did not transfer it to the conducting score. Handel also put the syllable "men" on beat four of the soprano part here, probably an error.

▮ P. 249 ▮

6) Measure 118. Text has been editorially added to the alto and tenor, based on the underlay in measures 75, 85, 105, and 112.

▮ P. 250 ▮

7) Measure 129. This is the proper text distribution for the alto part, according to the autograph score.

▮ P. 251 ▮

8) Measures 138-139. Spicker had the wrong text underlay here. This is the proper rhythm and text distribution according to the autograph score.

▮ P. 252 ▮

9) Measure 152. The autograph and conducting scores make clear that the syllable "men" should be on the last two eighth notes, not just the last one.

"Hallelujah"

Trumpet I in B♭

For the Lord God om-ni - po-tent reign - eth.

King of Kings,

No. 44 *Chorus*
"Hallelujah"

Trumpet I in D

For the Lord God om-ni-po-tent reign-eth.

King of Kings,

© MCMXCIII Roger Dean Publishing Co.

No. 44 *Chorus*
"Hallelujah"

For the Lord God om-ni-po-tent reign-eth.

King of Kings,

✦ ✦ ✦

Distinguished Major Works
from
Roger Dean Publishing Company

Christ Is Born . . . . J. Willcocks . . . . SATB CC122

Dixit Dominus . . . . Galuppi/Larson . . . . SSA HCMC108

English Christmas Festival. . . . H. Livingston. . . . . SATB CS903

For Unto Us . . . . G. Krapf. . . . . SATB CC112

Gloria . . . . Carcani/Larson . . . . SATB divisi CS138

Gloria . . . . Vivaldi/E. Thomas . . . . SATB CC96

Jephte . . . . Carissimi/Contino . . . . SATB HCMC107

Magnificat In G . . . . Pachelbel/W. Rodby . . . . . . SATB CS880

Mass In G . . . . Schubert/E. Thomas . . . . . . SATB CS865

Messiah. . . . . Handel/Van Camp. . . . . SATB 65/1001

Te Deum . . . . Mozart/W. Rodby . . . . SATB CS921